BIRDS
OF THE
BIBLE

A GUIDE FOR
BIBLE READERS
AND BIRDWATCHERS

BIRDS
OF THE
BIBLE

A GUIDE FOR
BIBLE READERS
AND BIRDWATCHERS

PETER
GOODFELLOW

In memory of my beloved wife, June,
who thought it was the best of me.

First published in the United Kingdom in 2013 by John Beaufoy Publishing,
11 Blenheim Court, 316 Woodstock Road, Oxford OX2 7NS, England
www.johnbeaufoy.com

10 9 8 7 6 5 4 3

ISBN 978-1-909612-14-3

Printed and bound in Malaysia by Times Offset (M) Sdn. Bhd.

Edited, designed and typeset by Gulmohur Press
Project management by Rosemary Wilkinson
Cartography by William Smuts

PAGE 2: BONELLI'S EAGLE; PAGE 3: EAGLE OWL

CONTENTS

PROLOGUE   'IN THE BEGINNING...'   6

CHAPTER I   THE CREATION OF BIRDS   12

CHAPTER II   HOW WELL DID PEOPLE KNOW THEIR BIRDS?   18

CHAPTER III   THE BIRD LIST IN LEVITICUS   26

CHAPTER IV   BIRDS FOR FOOD   44

CHAPTER V   BIRDS AND PARTICULAR PEOPLE   58

CHAPTER VI   JOB'S BIRDS   68

CHAPTER VII   BIRDS AND JESUS   80

CHAPTER VIII SINGING AND NESTING BIRDS   98

CHAPTER IX   THE MIGRATION OF BIRDS   116

CHAPTER X   EAGLES AND VULTURES   128

CHAPTER XI   BIRDS AND WORSHIP   148

EPILOGUE   FURTHER READING & ACKNOWLEDGEMENTS   158

INDEX   159

"IN THE BEGINNING..."

A
ll good "Where to watch..." bird books include descriptions of the landscape where birdwatchers should go. Our birdwatching trip through the Bible needs a few words about our destination, The Holy Land. Not everyone will be able to see the Promised Land at first hand, but some idea of an environment that is so very different from our own and the variety of birds which may be observed there, will hopefully revive memories of birds we have seen in the wild or in images from books or films, so that the scripture references to doves or ravens or eagles can be part of a real place, not just names on a page.

The land where the birds of the Bible lived does not fit neatly into a modern political map. Although for many years the Jews lived in Egypt and Babylon, most of their story takes place in "Palestine", and this is now covered by two modern nations – Israel and Jordan. The politics of the area today means that many people are very sensitive about who has the right to this bit of land or that. So in the pages that follow "Palestine" means the land in the Bible, "Jordan" refers to just the river or the valley that bears its name and "Israel" refers to the ancient name of the Jewish northern kingdom that lay north of Jerusalem, as opposed to Judah that lay to the south.

A glance at a map shows clearly that the birds of the Bible are confined to a narrow country in the south-east corner of the Mediterranean Sea. Since ancient times, Palestine (or Canaan as it was called before that) has been a narrow corridor, between the landmass of Arabia and Southeast Asia and the Mediterranean Sea. This was an ideal route for traders travelling between Egypt and Asia Minor, and for armies of leaders in search of enlarging their empires. It was – and is – a territory that was often fought over.

A closer look at the land reveals a definite north-south orientation of highlands and lowlands, and their related climatic and vegetation zones. Here is a land that varies between the harsh, barren landscape of the south, to the land "flowing with milk and honey" (Job, ch. 20, v. 17) west of the Jordan, to the majestic Mount Hermon in the north. For most of Palestine, geographers say the area has a Mediterranean climate. There is a marked dry season from mid-June to mid-September. The winter rain is not so regular, and appreciable rainfall may not occur till after Christmas. The summers are hot. Average temperatures in

LEBANON

JEBEL LIBAN

JEBEL ESH-SHARQI

Sayda ○

Jazzin ○

○ Damascus

Tyre ○

▲ *Mt Hermon*

SYRIA

Hula Nature Reserve ●

○ El Qunaytirah

Nahariyya ○

'Akko ○

*Lake Tiberias
(Sea of Galilee)*

GOLAN

Capernaum ○

HEIGHTS

MEDITERRANEAN

Haifa ○
▲
Mt Carmel

Tiberias ○

Nazareth ○

SEA

○ Afula

Yarmuk

○ Dar'a

Jenino ○

Hadera ○

Netanya ○

○ Tulkarm

GILEAD

Ajlun ○

○ Mafráq

Nablus ○

Jordan

Zarqa

Herzliyya ○

WEST BANK

○ Zarqa

Tel Aviv ○

Ba'al Hazor
▲

Rishon le Zion ○

Rehovot ○

Jericho ○

○ Amman

Ashdod ○

○ Jerusalem

○ Madaba

Ashqelon ○

Bethlehem ○

GAZA
STRIP

Hebron ○

DEAD SEA

Gaza ○

Mujib

Khan Yunis ○

Beersheba ○

○ Mazra

○ Quatrana

ISRAEL

○ Dimona

Wadi el Jeib

○ Tafila

N e g e v

EGYPT

JORDAN

Wadi al Araba

○ Petra

ESH SHARA

○ Ma'an

El Kuntilla ○

Yotvata ○

▲ *Jebel Ram*

Eilat ○
○ Aqaba

Gulf of Aqaba

0 ⊏⊐⊏⊐⊏⊐ 50 miles

0 ⊏⊐⊏⊐ 50 km

Topographical map of Israel

the Jordan Valley from May to October are usually well over 30°C/86°F; winters are much cooler, below 10°C/50°F in December to February; in Jerusalem the average August temperature is 29°C/85°F, whereas in January it is only 8°C/47°F. Frost may then occur at night, and it may even snow in the south, as happened in the winter of 1991–1992 when banana plantations in Jericho were ruined. The temperature and rainfall vary greatly through the area because of the landscape; the western facing slopes are wetter than the eastern, and temperatures tend to increase the further one goes from the sea and further south.

Many years ago the Psalmist wrote: "the earth is full of your creatures"(Psalm 104, v. 24). This was certainly true in biblical times, when the landscape gave a great variety of habitats, even though the underlying rock was largely limestone or sandstone, except for the alluvial plain and Rift Valley. The lowlands behind the sand dunes of the coast are now orange groves, vineyards and fields of cereals and vegetables, but in ancient times there would have been large areas of marshland as well as settlements. The hill country still has extensive areas of wild flowers in spring and scrubland of Dwarf Oaks, Carob trees and Rockrose. This scrub can be very dense, particularly around Mount Carmel and on the hills around Galilee. The Rift Valley has vegetation the thickness of jungles and tropical heat in summer to go with it! The heat and the water create a lush, green ribbon of vegetation that closely follows the river and consists of Tamarisk, and Christ's Thorn (*Paliurus spina-christi)* that can grow to a height of 15 m (over 45 ft). Many waterbirds are still found north of Galilee at the Hula (or Huleh) nature reserve. It is a marsh of papyrus and other plants, but is only a fraction of its ancient size because much has been drained for farmland. The Negev Desert in the south is never completely bare and sandy as one often thinks a desert is; the hills may be bare and stony, but many wadis (valleys which may have a stream in the rainy season) and hollows have stunted bushes, and a good rainy season will bring a flush of grass and flowers.

The Bible often speaks of "forest", but this most likely referred to the areas of impenetrable scrub; true forest trees such as Cedar and Cypress which were used for buildings and ships had to be imported from Phoenicia and Lebanon. The frequent references to "forest" do indicate, however, that trees (and associated fires) were much more widespread in the past than they are today, as we read, for example, in God's words: "I will kindle fires in your forests" (Jeremiah, ch. 21, v. 14), and "every animal of the forest is mine" (Psalm 50, v. 10). It is interesting to note that when The Ark of the Covenant was recaptured from the Philistines, it was the men of "the village of the woods", Kiriath Jearim, who rescued it (1 Samuel, ch. 6, v. 21).

A contrast to the lowlands and their lush vegetation is Mount Hermon in the far north. Its summit at 2,814 m (9,232 ft) is now actually in Syria. It is snow-capped all year round, and today the Israeli slopes are a winter ski resort. In biblical times and earlier its majestic appearance was well known, and the Cedars which grew on its slopes were written about by Ezekiel. Its name may mean "sacred or forbidden place". Mountains all over the world have been held in awe, and perhaps this is why the Psalmist speaks rapturously of it:

PSALM 89, v.12   *You created the north and the south;*
Tabor and Hermon sing for joy at your name.

The variety of landscapes gave much shelter to birds and beasts. The evidence that it was rather different from today is given in the many references to "the birds of the air".

HOOPOE

Bee-eaters at nesting colony

Notwithstanding the greater area under crops today and the rarity of some species that were reported in the scriptures, ornithologists have established that nearly 500 species have been recorded in the modern state of Israel. Today the pilgrim or birdwatcher will be thrilled by Bee-eaters, Hoopoes and songbirds and we will read about many of them in the chapters that follow. Palestine's "beasts of the forest" included lions, wolves, crocodiles, gazelles, deer and foxes, as well as the smaller creatures in this detailed list:

Four things on earth are small,
yet they are extremely wise:
Ants are creatures of little strength,
yet they store up their food in the summer;

≈ PROVERBS   *conies [the Rock Hyrax or Rock badger]*
CH. 30, VV. 24 – 28   *are creatures of little power,*
yet they make their home in the crags; locusts have no king,
yet they advance together in ranks;
a lizard can be caught with the hand,
yet it is found in kings' palaces. ≈

Lions, wolves and crocodiles are extinct there now, but the rest remain, and the visitor who knows where to look and is quietly observant, will see them and the birds, and will agree with the Psalmist that the earth is indeed full of God's creatures.

ROCK HYRAX

CHAPTER I

THE CREATION OF BIRDS

The Bible records that on the fifth day of Creation God said, "Let the waters teem with living creatures, and let birds fly above the earth across the expanse of the sky. So God created the great creatures of the sea and every living and moving thing with which the water teems, according to their kinds, and every winged bird according to its kind. And God saw that it was good. God blessed them and said, 'Be fruitful and increase in number and fill the water in the seas, and let the birds increase on the earth.'" (Genesis, ch. 1, vv. 20–22). The birds have indeed been fruitful and have increased. Today, they are found on every continent, in every habitat, from the snowy wastes of Antarctica to the steaming hot rainforests around the Equator. Scientists believe there are about 10,000 species; new ones are discovered every year in remote places; and others which once were thought to be a single species with slight variations in plumage or behaviour, are now known to be separate species thanks to the study of their DNA.

Further on we read, "Now the Lord God had formed out of the ground all the beasts of the field and all the birds of the air. He brought them to the man to see what he would name them; and whatever the man called each living creature, that was its name. So the man gave names to all the livestock, the birds of the air and the beasts of the field" (Genesis, ch. 2, vv. 19–20). Part of Mankind's stewardship of Creation (God said, "Let us make man in our image, in our likeness, and let them rule over...the birds of the air" Genesis, ch. 2, v. 26) has indeed resulted in birds being named carefully by peoples and nations throughout the world. Wonderfully today, we find that no matter where we are in the world we can learn what the local people call the birds with which they are familiar. Peoples who live in harmony with their surroundings understand how valuable trees, plants, animals and birds are to their own existence, and thus know them by name.

The Australian aborigines have the wonderful Dreamtime (their religious time) stories about the animals and birds they know well. They have their own names for Australian birds, for example the Eulayhi peoples' Gooloo, Deereeree and Galah, and when I was in Queensland, these birds were called Australian Magpie, Willie Wagtail and Galah – the small pink cockatoo. Laurens van der Post narrates a splendid story about a Kalahari Bushman in his book *The Heart of the Hunter*. A Bushman the author knew well once told

Swift (top) and swallow

him about the "person with wings" who cries clearly, *Quick! Quick! Quick! Honey! Quick!* That bird was calling for its "friend", the Ratel, or Honey Badger, to come and dig out a beehive that it had found so that both could enjoy the feast of honey. What is more, the Bushmen have learned from birds and animals and can imitate their calls, and are thus able to lure the Ratel to open a hive, overcome the bees with a powerful smell, so that the men can harvest the honeycomb. Laurens van der Post sees this as a parable which has stood the test of time: "... in the first language of things, honey is the supreme symbol of wisdom, since wisdom is the sweetness of the strength that comes to the spirit dedicated to the union of warring elements of life". The Bushmen do indeed "rule over" these creatures with gentleness and wisdom. Today, we know the "person with wings" as a member of the Honeyguide family, a dozen species of which live in Africa, south of the Sahara. In South Africa, in Afrikaans, it is called *Heuningwyser*. The scientific family name of many of them (the genus) is well chosen – *Indicator*. Honeyguides are not found in Israel, but the biblical Israelites did have names for their birds too, as we shall see.

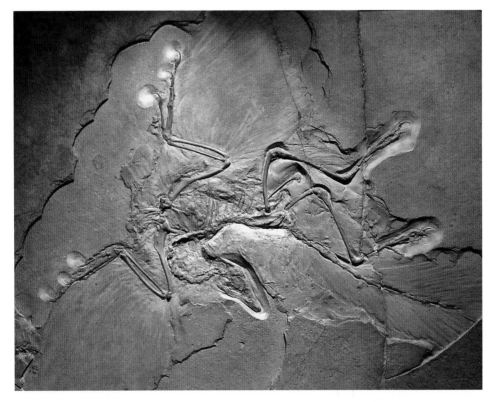

FOSSIL OF ARCHAEOPTERYX

The writer of Genesis had a God-given insight into the order in which life on Earth came about. Whether we believe that it all happened in six days, or slowly over the millennia, we read that birds appeared on Earth after the trees, plants and sea creatures. The study of fossils has revealed that birds first appeared in the Jurassic Period (180–135 million years ago). Scientists were able to work this out after the discovery of a fossil feather in 1860, and in 1861 of a complete bird skeleton, from a quarry of fine-grained limestone in Solnhofen, Bavaria, Germany. This fossil became known as *Archaeopteryx lithographica* – the first name means "ancient wing", and the second honours the fact that slabs of limestone were used in the printing process called lithography (many of this book's illustrations were originally printed by this method). This bird was believed to have flown about 150,000,000 years ago. Other land-based and seaside fossil species have been named since. As the hymn-writer William Cowper wrote:

> *God moves in a mysterious way*
> *His wonders to perform;*
> *He plants his footsteps in the sea,*
> *And rides upon the storm.*

> *Deep in the unfathomable mines*
> *Of never-failing skill*
> *He treasures up his bright designs,*
> *And works his sovereign will.*

Cowper wrote this in 1773, long before Darwin published his *Origin of Species* in 1859. The wonderful number and variety of birds, from tiny hummingbirds to huge eagles, from black and white penguins to multicoloured pheasants, helps many people believe that they are indeed evidence of Creation's mystery, wonder and skilful design.

The birds of Creation particularly inspired the Old Testament writers to describe the world in which the people lived. Later, Jesus did the same in His teachings (see Chapter 7, *Birds and Jesus*). A thousand or more years after Genesis was written, an anonymous author wrote The Wisdom of Solomon. This is not in the Hebrew Bible, but was accepted by Jerome for his Latin translation that we know as the Vulgate Bible. It is still part of the canon for Roman Catholics and many Orthodox groups, but is only accepted in the Apocrypha in the Protestant Bible. The author was fascinated by the passing of time and the lack of signs to show what creatures had lived before in that place:

 CH. 5, V. 11

When a bird has flown through the air, there is no token of her way to be found, but the light air being beaten with the stroke of her wings, and parted with the violent noise and motion of them; it is passed through, and afterwards there is no sign in the air to be found of where she went.

Today, we still say, "Oh, how time flies!" But for most of us our thoughts soon move on to other things, and we do not allow our imaginations to explore the thought of flying time as the writer did centuries ago.

Bird sounds greatly affected the writers in ancient Palestine. Much of what we can read in the Bible today concerns the mournful sounds of the owl and the dove, two birds we shall consider more carefully later (Chapters 3 and 5). But the sounds of birds singing is recorded too, lifting the spirits of the writer and reader (see also Chapter 8):

SONG OF SONGS
CH. 2, VV. 11-12

See! The winter is past;
the rains are over and gone.
Flowers appear on the earth;
the season of singing has come,
the cooing of doves
is heard in our land.

GRACEFUL PRINIA,
A COMMON
SONG BIRD

Whether King Solomon wrote this love song as is traditionally thought, or it was simply about him, does not spoil the poem's romantic imagery which is timeless and as understandable in our culture today as it was in the Middle East hundreds of years before Christ. Apart from the cooing of doves, this and the next reference are the only ones to the songs of other birds generally. The most likely songster is the Yellow-vented Bulbul that is found throughout the Middle East. It is a resident in Israel, a bird of gardens, plantations and oases and is very common wherever trees and bushes are to found and so is even seen in villages and towns. Its bold, oft-repeated song, proclaiming that it has a territory, is

YELLOW-VENTED
BULBUL

especially to be heard in spring, in March and April, starting before sunrise. I have listened to one in April, singing from a television aerial overlooking the Pool of Bethesda, in the old part of Jerusalem.

Of all the writings in the Old and New Testaments, the composition that most closely records the author's wonder at God's Creation is Psalm 104. This does not repeat the description of the order of Creation, but is a hymn to the Creator praising the wonders that the Psalmist sees before him – the heavens, the seas, the valleys, the mountains are all there, richly filled with plants, animals, food, and "The birds of the air nest by the waters; they sing among the branches...The trees of the Lord are well watered, the Cedars of Lebanon that he planted. There the birds make their nests; the stork has its home in the pine trees" (vv. 12, 16, 17). Apart from the words that describe the glory of Creation, the carefully controlled structure of the psalm is a further sign of the Psalmist's sense of wonder and desire to praise the Lord. The main part of the psalm begins with the heavens (v. 1) and ends with the seas (v. 26), the two elements that, in his experience, hold the earth where he sees the splendours of Creation.

As we stop to consider the world around us – springtime primroses, a rainbow, snow-capped hills, the first Swallow of the new year – we can well understand why the Psalmist sang God's praises like "the birds of the air".

CHAPTER 11

HOW WELL DID PEOPLE KNOW THEIR BIRDS?

The first ornithologist to take an active interest in the birds of the Holy Land was the Victorian clergyman, Canon Henry Baker Tristram. After a curacy in Devon and later as vicar in County Durham, he rose to be canon of Durham Cathedral. Ill health from tuberculosis forced the canon to spend long periods of time abroad, in warmer, drier climes, such as Palestine. His explorations and studies resulted in several books, particularly the groundbreaking *Natural History of the Bible* (1867) and *Flora and Fauna of Palestine* (1884). Notwithstanding ill health, he was happily married, celebrated his golden wedding anniversary and lived till he was 83! He died in 1906. He was a well-known figure in Palestine and two birds have been named after him. Tristram's Serin is a close relative of the Canary, and has a song to match. It breeds commonly on Mount Hermon where traditionally Jesus was Transfigured (see St Matthew, ch. 17; St Mark, ch. 9; St Luke, ch. 9). The other bird is Tristram's Grackle that the Jews today call "Tristramit". It is a relative of the familiar Starling and has a limited distribution in the Arabian Peninsula; however, in more recent times it has spread north to near Jericho. Pilgrims to the Holy Land today may see it as closely as I did at the fortress of Masada overlooking the Dead Sea. The Essenes, who were a Jewish religious sect, had a monastic-style settlement at Qumran to the north of Masada. Some scholars say that John the Baptist and Jesus may have had links with them. So, who knows, the cousins may have seen these distinctive, red-winged, black birds as well.

TRISTRAM'S SERIN

That the Hebrews were familiar with many birds, and often referred to them figuratively to emphasize and explain aspects of their own behaviour, is revealed in many biblical references. However, it is only after we put their knowledge into a worldwide context that we can appreciate how accurate their observations were.

Among the earliest bird records we have are from the Stone Age. Some recognizable birds are evident in the cave paintings of the Aurignacian people of 18,000 to 11,000 years ago at Lascaux near Montignac, France; and there are even more species from 6,000 to 4,000 years ago in Spain.

Today we, who carry field guides wherever we go to help us identify birds, often tend to believe that accurate identification is a modern skill, aided by our easy access to binoculars and telescopes. But the ancient Egyptians as long ago as 3,000 BC were careful observers and splendid artists. At the time when Joseph was interpreting the dreams of the baker and the butler (Genesis, ch. 40), the Egyptians were familiar with waterside birds such as herons, the Sacred Ibis and geese, and land birds like Swallows, shrikes, the Hoopoe and birds of prey. We know this because accurate representations of these birds and others still exist today on

TRISTRAM'S
GRACKLE

wall paintings, papyrus scrolls and sculptures. I am sure that Joseph and the two servants knew exactly which birds featured in their dreams and which ones ate the baker's bread and other baked goods – sparrows or doves most probably. Even worse, the birds that were "to eat the baker's flesh" were certainly well known. The Griffon Vulture, a very large scavenger of carrion, was the visual representation of the Egyptian goddess of heaven, Nekhebt, and a dramatic painting of the vulture in flight, dating from 1485 BC, is on the wall of Queen Hat-shepsut's temple near Thebes. Joseph must surely have been familiar with the birds the Egyptians knew because as the Pharaoh said "...there is no-one so discerning and wise as you" (Genesis, ch. 41 v. 39). The New International Study Bible tells us that Moses was born in 1526 BC and died in 1406 BC. The Pharaoh's daughter who rescued Moses as a baby may later have been Queen Hat-shepsut. Having been brought up in the royal household, Moses would have known their gods and hieroglyphic writing, and no doubt saw the birds which were often depicted in the pictograms in the countryside. The Sacred Ibis was the symbol of Thoth, the god of learning, science and art; and the Peregrine Falcon for Horus, the chief god of united Egypt. All Moses' beliefs completely changed after his experience at the Burning Bush (Exodus, ch. 3), which was a time of enlightenment, bringing him understanding of the one true God of Abraham, Isaac and Jacob.

Closer to the time of Christ, we have the Greek facts and myths about birds. The people in ancient times lived closer to nature than we do, even if they were residents of a town or city. Almost every aspect of life in ancient Greece was affected by birds. Their philosophical and scientific studies, religion, deep belief in omens, weather forecasting, food, as well as the fact that birds were kept as pets are all recorded in the books of Aristotle (died 322 BC), Aristophanes (fourth century BC), the playwright who wrote *The Birds*, Aelian (died 235 AD) and others. Aristotle, who was tutor to Alexander the Great, recorded about 120 species that can be recognized today from his descriptions. Artists of the period illustrated vultures, cranes, owls, herons, Ravens, swans, Swallows and songbirds on sculptures and ceramics.

By the time of Christ, the Hebrews who had lived long among the Egyptians, were now immersed in Greek culture. The use of the Greek language was widespread among the educated. All the writers of the New Testament wrote in Greek, or their scribes did. At that time Palestine was under the control of another great civilization – the Romans, builders of arterial roads and splendid edifices. The early Christians no doubt learnt the skills of the thinkers, artists and writers of their time, although this is illustrated at a later period than the Bible texts, at the Byzantine church at Tabgha near Capernaum. The church is situated on the site where it is believed Christ fed the five thousand (St Matthew, ch. 6; St Mark, ch. 14). It dates from the fourth century AD, was enlarged in the fifth century, was destroyed by the

PEREGRINE

SACRED IBIS

CORMORANTS

Muslim invaders, and rediscovered in 1932. The ruins contain the finest floor mosaics in Israel. One depicts a long-necked swan or a goose, and two cormorants in their typical wing-drying pose, together with beasts, fish and ribbons of flowers. The cormorant in the mosaic is a small bird and looks like a reasonable representation of the Pygmy Cormorant, not the Great Cormorant which is now, and probably always was, an uncommon bird in Palestine. The Pygmy Cormorant used to be a common winter visitor to the Hula wetlands north of Galilee, where it also bred until the 1950s, before they were drained. If the translation of Leviticus 11 is right – and it is disputed – the Cormorant was an unclean bird and could not be eaten. Whether the translation is right or wrong, it is tempting to think that Peter and the other New Testament fishermen often saw these birds on the Sea of Galilee. Another mosaic shows a splendid cock Peacock, a bird introduced in ancient times from Asia.

Although this historical evidence that past civilizations were very aware of the birds that lived around them is encouraging, the Bible record is actually rather slim. In all there are about 300 references to birds. They range from the mention of "bird/birds" as a general term, to very specific descriptions. The former in the original Hebrew uses one of two general words. "Oph" is for birds and other flying creatures like insects and it is used in the Genesis story. The other general word is "tsippor" which usually denotes game birds, like the "bird from the snare of the fowler" (Proverbs, ch. 6, v. 5), or perching birds, like the one "alone on a roof" (Psalm 102,

v. 7). Moses' wife's name, Zipporah, is derived from this word because she was a bird-like delight for her parents. It is amusing to know today that in England, a Westcountry boy may say to his girlfriend, "Hello ma bird!" In the New Testament Greek there are also two words for birds. Birds in general are "peteinon" as in St Matthew, ch. 6, v. 26: "Look at the birds of the air; they do not sow or reap or store away in barns". The second, "orneon" refers to flesh-eating birds like vultures, as in the description of the destruction of Babylon that is "the haunt of every unclean and detestable bird"(Revelation, ch. 18, v. 2).

Many birds are named specifically, as we shall see, but since a number of the original Hebrew names are not understood today, the birds cannot be accurately identified. When Alice Parmelee published her definitive *All the Birds of the Bible* in 1959 she quoted extensively from Dr G.R. Driver's list of transliterations and suggested translations that he had published in 1955. Many of these names found their way into modern Bible translations. Further research today has thrown even more light on the identity of several Bible birds. A comparison of the names in one verse, Jeremiah, ch. 8, v. 7, reveals the problem we still have if we compare just six well-known English translations:

Authorised Version	Good News Bible	New English Bible	New Revised Standard Version	New International Version	New King James Version
1611	*1976*	*1961*	*1989*	*1987*	*1982*
stork	stork	stork	stork	stork	stork
turtle (dove)	dove	dove	Turtle Dove	dove	Turtle Dove
crane	swallow	swift	crane	swift	swift
swallow	thrush	wryneck	swallow	thrush	swallow

The birds in the first two lines are certainly identified: the Stork and the dove (Shakespeare wrote of the Turtle in several plays and always meant the Turtle Dove; it is named after its call – *turr turrrr turrrrr*). Non-birdwatchers today still confuse the Swallow and Swift, so that difference is understandable; but the jump from "thrush" to "crane" is more puzzling. We will read about them all in more detail later.

The famous list of unclean birds in Leviticus chapter 11 is even more problematical and will be discussed in Chapter 3. Here, we are simply comparing Dr Driver's list of some of the species with the names in a modern Israeli bird book, *Checklist of the Birds of Israel*, published in 1987 by the Society for the Protection of Nature in Israel and Tel Aviv University.

LONG-EARED OWL   HONEY BUZZARD

Let us first look at names that show some agreement:

Dr Driver's List 1955		**Checklist of the Birds of Israel 1987**	
Hebrew	*English*	*Hebrew*	*English*
kos	Tawny Owl	kos hehorvot	Little Owl
yanshuph	Screech Owl	yanshuf ezim	Long-eared owl
		yanshuf sadot	Short-eared Owl
dukipheth	Hoopoe	dukhipat	Hoopoe
chasidah	stork	hasidah	stork
nesher	Griffon Vulture	nesher	Griffon Vulture
peres	Bearded Vulture	peres	Bearded Vulture
daah	kite	daya	kite
oreb	Raven	orev	Raven
anaphah	heron	anafit or anafat	heron

Interestingly, Dr Driver believed "shachaph" was the Long-eared Owl, whereas the New Revised Standard Version calls it a "sea gull"; the latter is more likely given the *Checklist's* words for owl above, and "shahaf" for all the gulls. Other "unclean" birds listed in Dr Driver's transliteration can be traced in the modern list, but with a different interpretation:

Dr Driver's List 1955		Checklist of the Birds of Israel 1987	
Hebrew	*English*	*Hebrew*	*English*
racham	Osprey	raham	Egyptian Vulture
shalak	Fisher Owl	shalakh	Osprey
tishemeth	Little Owl	tinshemet	Barn (or Screech) Owl
tachmas	Short-eared Owl	tahmass	Nightjar
ayyah	falcon or buzzard	ayat	Honey buzzard
ozniyyah	Short-toed Eagle	ozniya shehora	Black Vulture

It is interesting to note that the New Revised Standard Version translation follows the *Checklist*'s names for "racham" and "tachmas".

There can be no doubt that the early Hebrews had an extensive knowledge of the birds of the Promised Land. Very early on their laws (preserved in the books of Leviticus and Deuteronomy) declared exactly which birds were unclean, that is, were not fit to eat (chapter 3), and those that were, by implication, good food. Large birds naturally caught their attention best, but small, perching birds also feature in the biblical records as we shall discover. Perhaps, what was most important was the symbolic role of birds as part of the people's sacrificial offerings (chapter 11) and as signs of God's protection and care (chapters 5 and 7).

Although the passage of time has not helped us match certain names with some birds, clearly some of the ancient bird names have lived for 3,000 years or more, a wonderful testimony to the careful way that God's Chosen People understood God's will: "He brought them to the man to see what he would name them; and whatever the man called each living creature, that was its name. So the man gave names to.... the birds of the air" (Genesis, ch. 2, vv. 19–20).

NIGHTJAR

CHAPTER **III**

THE BIRD LIST IN LEVITICUS

When Noah's Ark at last came to rest as the Flood went down, Noah brought his family and all the animals and birds out onto the dry land:

 GENESIS
CH. 8, vv. 20-21

Then Noah built an altar to the Lord and, taking some of all the clean animals and clean birds, he sacrificed burnt offerings on it. The Lord smelled the pleasing aroma...

This is the earliest story in the Bible of people worshipping God with a sacrifice, and figuratively, the "pleasing aroma" is a way of saying that God was pleased with his children's worship. In the Genesis story God had given mankind the privilege and responsibility of looking after Creation. Then the creatures were given names, and thirdly, God limited what His Chosen People could eat.

Many tribal peoples through the ages have recognized that blood is the stuff of life. Blood is precious and holy, and so was, from ancient times, a rich part of sacrificial ceremonies; sometimes it was actually drunk by some communities to give participants strength and a strong life. In certain cases, the blood of two men was intermingled to seal a bargain or a vow. The Hebrews too, as they established laws to guide their lives, had a firm view of what blood meant to them. In the laws governing sacrifices we read that, depending on the reason the offering was being made, the animal's or bird's blood had to be carefully spilt or sprinkled or poured or spread. For a Guilt Offering we read that the slaughtered animal's "blood is to be sprinkled against the altar on all sides" (Leviticus, ch. 7, v. 2). Life is from God. Blood is life. So blood is holy, and to eat blood was an offence against God, and the offender was considered ritually "unclean". Therefore, the Law said, "Wherever you live, you must not eat the blood of any bird or animal. If anyone eats blood that person must be cut off from his people" (Leviticus, ch. 7, vv. 26–27). The meat from which the blood has been drained is "kosher". The Law is emphasized even more strongly later:

Kestrel

LEVITICUS
CH. 17, vv. 13-16

The Lord said to Moses, "Any Israelite or any alien living among you who hunts any animal or bird that may be eaten must drain out the blood and cover it with earth, because the life of every creature is its blood. That is why I have said to the Israelites, 'You must not eat the blood of any creature, because the life of every creature is its blood.'"

The laws that Moses received from God governed the whole life of the people. If a person did something wrong, or in other words had sinned, he or she…

LEVITICUS
CH. 5, vv. 5-7

…must confess in what way he has sinned and, as a penalty for the sin he has committed, he must bring to the Lord a female lamb or goat from the flock as a sin offering; and the priest shall make atonement for him for his sin. If he cannot afford a lamb, he is to bring two doves or two young pigeons to the Lord as a penalty for his sin – one for a sin offering and the other for a burnt offering.

OSPREY

Birds were thus at the heart of Israel's life. They were at the climax of the people's daily life at their main meal, because the Law stated very clearly which birds were "unclean" and could not be part of food. The distinction between "clean" and "unclean" goes back to the story of Noah when God told him to take into the Ark a pair each of clean and unclean creatures. Now "clean" and "unclean" here do not refer to dirty or diseased food as opposed to good, tasty food, but were a way of preserving and demonstrating the sanctity of Israel as God's Chosen People: "I am the Lord your God, consecrate yourselves and be holy, because I am holy" (Leviticus, ch. 11, v. 44).

As a sure way of ensuring that they did not defile themselves by eating any creature which was "unclean", the books of the Law clearly list the mammals, reptiles, insects and birds which should not be eaten or touched. So we are led to the longest, most famous list of birds in the Bible, in Leviticus, which is then repeated in Deuteronomy:

LITTLE EGRETS, ONE OF SEVERAL MEMBERS OF THE HERON FAMILY IN ISRAEL

≈ LEVITICUS
CH. 11, VV. 13-19
NIV

These are the birds you are to detest and not eat because they are detestable: the eagle, the vulture, the black vulture, the red kite, any kind of black kite, any kind of raven, the horned owl, the screech owl, the gull, any kind of hawk, the little owl, the cormorant, the great owl, the white owl, the desert owl, the osprey, the stork, any kind of heron, the hoopoe and the bat. ≈

or

 GOOD NEWS
BIBLE

*These are the birds you shall regard as vermin, and
for this reason they shall not be eaten: the Griffon
Vulture (or eagle), the Black Vulture, and the
Bearded Vulture (or ossifrage); the kite and every
kind of falcon; every kind of crow (or Raven), the
Desert-owl, the Short-eared Owl, the Long-eared
Owl, and every kind of hawk; the Tawny Owl, the
Fisher-owl, and the Screech-owl; the Little Owl, the
Horned Owl, the Osprey, the Stork (or Heron), every
kind of Cormorant, the Hoopoe and the bat.*

Nineteen species or categories of birds are listed here, in
whatever translation you read. There are basically three
groups: birds of prey, waterbirds and two perching birds
one of which, the Hoopoe, seems on the face of it, the odd
one out. I am sure the Hebrews knew that a bat was not a
bird – but bats do fly, they do eat insects that are unclean,
and so they eat blood and are therefore "unclean".

It is quite easy to understand why many of these birds
were forbidden. They are hunters. They spill blood, and
as we have seen blood is life. Animals that have eaten
blood, therefore, are "unclean" because the Jews were
themselves forbidden to eat blood, as we have seen in
Leviticus, chapter 7. The command was forcefully
repeated in chapter 17, vv. 13–14:

BARN OWL

*Any Israelite or any foreigner living among you
who hunts an animal or bird that may be eaten
must drain out the blood and cover it with earth
because the life of every creature is its blood.*

We have already discovered in Chapter 2 that it is not easy for scholars today to identify
some of the ancient birds. I now propose to write in greater detail about the birds we can be

sure, or reasonably sure, about, based on the Hebrew names as mentioned in *Young's Analytical Concordance*, the most commonly used modern translation, with help from the modern *Checklist of the Birds of Israel* and the New International Version translation.

The first group contains the large birds of prey whose mighty wingspan would have made them a very noticeable sight in the sky. Many translations list the eagle first, as a translation for *nesher* which we have seen is more usually the word for vulture now (page 24). Clearly vultures are in the list anyway with the name *peres*; and there are many references to owls. That eagles and vultures were not clearly identified is not surprising. There are five vultures on the Israeli bird list and ten

GRIFFON VULTURE

eagles. The confusion over some of the owls is probably because they are rarely seen clearly by day, but they could with practice be differentiated by their calls. However, this may be difficult too, for all ten species. We will consider these birds of prey (and the others) from a birdwatching point of view in this chapter, and look at their descriptive and symbolic use in Chapter 10.

I well remember standing by the ruins of Qumran by the Dead Sea looking north, straining my eyes through my binoculars, to try to identify an eagle. Almost any eagle there would be something special, and very different from Britain's two species – the Golden and the Sea Eagles. Eventually the bird came close enough to be identified as an immature Bonelli's Eagle. It is now rather rare in Israel but was quite widespread until the 1950s; thereafter its population was decimated by poisoning from agro-chemicals in the food chain.

The Short-toed or Snake Eagle is a common migrant through Israel, and a few pairs stay to breed in the Judean and Negev deserts. This eagle is twice damned, if indeed it is meant by the "ozniyyah" as Dr Driver suggests (although the Good News Bible quotation above translates it as the Black Vulture which, according to the *Checklist*, is called "ozniya shehora" in Hebrew today). It is a flesh eater, so it eats blood, but worse still is that up to 70 per cent of its main prey are snakes, another forbidden, "unclean" creature. Although a large bird with a wingspan of up to 178 cm (74 in), it may be seen hovering in the wind over rough ground looking for food.

Bearded Vulture

| Birds of the Bible

The time when the Hebrews of old would most likely have seen "eagles swooping down on their prey"(Job, ch. 9, v. 26) was in autumn when large numbers pass through Palestine on their way to winter in East Africa. Two species in particular, in modern times anyway, have been especially common and there is no reason to believe that this has changed. The eagles of the genus *Aquila* are among the largest, our Golden Eagle included. Of the two species, birdwatchers counted nearly 142,000 Lesser Spotted Eagles passing south at Kefar Kassem between the end of August and mid-October in 1983. This eagle has a wingspan of up to 168 cm (70 in). Even larger is the Tawny or Steppe Eagle that has broad, dark brown wings spanning up to 190 cm (79 in) and is a dramatic sight in the sky. It, too, is seen in large numbers on migration. In southern Israel at Eilat c.29,000 were identified passing north in the spring of 1977. With so many of them drifting by on thermals of warm air, or hunting by the wayside, it is no wonder that the writer of Proverbs, maybe Solomon himself, wrote:

 PROVERBS
CH. 23, V. 5

Cast but a glance at riches, and they are gone,
for they will surely sprout wings
and fly off to the sky like an eagle.

Perhaps the most splendid mention of an eagle (but see Chapter 10 to help you make up your mind) is also from Proverbs, where the writer declares:

PROVERBS
CH. 30, VV. 18-19

There are three things that are too amazing for me,
four that I do not understand:
the way of an eagle in the sky,
the way of a snake on a rock,
the way of a ship on the high seas,
and the way of a man with a maiden.

I am sure that eagles were a rich part of the Hebrews' daily experience.

The second group of large, flesh-eating, blood-spilling birds that are unclean are vultures. The most startling and accurate reference to these carrion feeders is found in Jesus' dramatic statement when He was talking to the disciples on the Mount of Olives a little time before the Passover. In St Matthew's Gospel, Jesus is reported to have hinted at the destruction of Jerusalem, which did indeed happen in AD 70. Excavations in the late 1960s even unearthed some of the stones that Jesus said would be thrown down. He was also trying to tell the disciples that when He came again and when the Coming of the Kingdom would happen, false Christs and false prophets would appear, thus the disciples must always be on their guard. Christ's appearance, however, will be as obvious as the gathering of vultures around a carcass (St Matthew, ch. 24, v. 28). St Luke (ch. 17, v. 37) records the same statement to illustrate the time of His Second Coming, the Parousia as it is called in Christian doctrine. But the disciples, still not understanding, asked, "Where, Lord?", and Jesus replied, "Where there is a dead body, there the vultures will gather". Neither the disciples nor we know in advance when the Second Coming will be, but it will be obvious when it does happen. Jesus' illustration may seem to us a rather gruesome way to explain the truth, but to the Hebrews it would have been natural to see such a sight. Vultures are communal feeders and one or two at a carcass will soon attract others, as tourists on African safaris know only too well. It is clear that something important is happening when the vultures gather.

The biggest species in the region are the well-named Black, Lappet-faced and Griffon Vultures. All are huge, powerful birds with wingspans of up to 290 cm (10 ft). The Black Vulture is now a rare migrant but Canon Tristram recorded its breeding in the cliffs of the Arbel near the Sea of Galilee in the late 19th century. The Lappet-faced Vulture has decreased greatly in modern times; there may be only a few left in the Negev in the south of Israel. The Griffon Vulture today is most likely to be seen in the Golan Heights, the Judean Desert to the west of the Dead Sea and in the cliffs in the Negev. The first Griffon I ever saw was gliding past me at eye level as I stood on the top of the eastern edge of the fortress at Masada. If any of the over 900 Jewish men, women and children who had been besieged in the fortress by the Romans in AD 74, saw one like I did, I can well imagine what thoughts of death they might have had. The siege ended that year with the mass suicide of all the Jews. All these vultures have decreased in modern times as settlements have become cleaner, farming more modernized in the kibbutzim and poisons spread to kill rodents, wild boars and jackals. These poisons in the food chain accumulate in the vultures' bodies and eventually kill them. This desperate state prevails in India today afflicting vultures that have eaten dead cattle that still have traces of medicine that had been administered for their good health, but which has been proved to be toxic for the vultures.

For the early Hebrews, the sight of many vultures at carcasses would have been a common sight after a battle or famine. King Jeroboam, who ruled the northern part of the divided kingdom after Solomon, was king

BLACK VULTURE

of a nation that deserted the One True God and worshipped Cananite idols. Ahijah, God's prophet then, spoke for God and said:

> "Because of this I am going to bring disaster on the House of Jeroboam. I will cut off from Jeroboam every last male in Israel - slave or free. I will burn up the house of Jeroboam as one burns dung, until it is gone. Dogs will eat those belonging to Jeroboam who die in the city, and the birds of the air will feed on those who die in the country. The Lord has spoken!"

1 KINGS
CH. 14, vv. 10-11

The Good News Bible translates the birds specifically as vultures, and as we have read, they are surely what God and Ahijah had in mind. About 300 years later the Psalmist wrote in a similar manner when he appealed on Israel's behalf for God's forgiveness and help, seeking judgement against the nations that had destroyed Israel and sent her people into exile:

> O God, the nations have invaded your inheritance;
> they have defiled your holy temple,
> they have reduced Jerusalem to rubble.
> They have given the dead bodies of your servants
> as food to the birds of the air,
> the flesh of your saints to the beasts of the earth.

PSALM
79, vv. 1-2

That the "birds of the air" here were indeed vultures is clear from the description of the food they ate – dead bodies. Their ability to find it is attested by Job:

> He dwells on a cliff and stays there at night; a rocky crag is his stronghold. From there he seeks out his food; his eyes detect it from afar.

JOB
CH. 39, vv. 28-29

According to an old Jewish commentary, the food is described as being as far away as Palestine when the bird is in Babylon! Vultures do find their food by sight, circling effortlessly several hundred feet up, until a carcass is sighted. The movement of one or two birds below will quickly attract others until dozens may gather at the body, pushing, squabbling, while they all try to get their fill. Some vultures have been seen to be so sated with food that they could not take off to fly to a roost. One dead Griffon was found to have 6 kg (13 lb) of meat in its crop.

But what is the "ossifrage" which is listed in the Authorised Version translation? The name is an adaptation of two Latin words meaning "bone-breaker". And that is exactly what this bird does. Today we know it as the Lammergeier or Bearded Vulture, a bird of rocky, mountainous regions. Its old name comes from its habit of picking up a bone from a carcass, flying up to 80 m (250 ft) or so, and dropping it on to rocks to be smashed, thus enabling the bird to get at the marrow and small bits of bone, which constitute 70 per cent of its diet. It is a very rare resident now in the Judean and Negev deserts. Its numbers have declined in modern times, as have the other vultures, yet Canon Tristram recorded its breeding in the cliffs near the Sea of Galilee. Although listed in the Authorised Version I can find no specific reference in the Bible to its amazing bone-breaking technique. Modern translations do translate "peres" as "vulture", but not as Dr Driver or the *Checklist* specifically do for this

SHORT-EARED
OWL

species, whose appearance (a rarity in Europe) and habits make it a bird which birdwatchers today particularly wish to see. The Bearded Vulture is still known as "peres" in Israel.

The listing of "kite" gives us another bird that feeds on carrion. The attractively coloured Red Kite was, according to Canon Tristram, common earlier but is now rare and seen only on passage. The Black Kite was quite a common breeding resident until the 1960s, but now only a few pairs can be found in the north. It is common on passage in spring and autumn, and widespread in Europe (not Britain or Scandinavia) and Asia. This is the bird that gathers in large numbers at rubbish heaps in the East. Although it is not referred to outside the Leviticus list, we can understand from its scavenging habits why the kites would have been considered "unclean". Its identity seems sure; the Hebrew word used is "daah" or "dayyah", and the modern Hebrew for the Black Kite is "daya mezuya" (other kites are "daya" plus an appropriate descriptor).

The Reverend Edward A. Armstrong in his well-known book *The Folklore of Birds* wrote:

> *People are apprehensive of anything which appears*
> *to have some human qualities without being*
> *human. Not only does the binocular vision of owls*
> *give them a resemblance to humanity but also*
> *the calls of some species are quasi-human. Their*
> *shrieks and hoots are often within the range of*
> *our own voices. Furthermore, nocturnal creatures*
> *naturally inspire fear ... Over Europe and Asia,*
> *and indeed, most of the world, the owl is, and long*
> *has been, a bird of witchcraft, death and doom.*

It is, therefore, no surprise to find six owls carefully named in the list of unclean birds. Isaiah describes the forthcoming destruction of Babylon in these terms:

ISAIAH
CH. 34, vv. 10-11

From generation to generation it will lie desolate;
the desert owl and screech owl will possess it ;
the great owl and raven will nest there.

"The precise identification of these birds is uncertain" say the editors of the New International Version. Suffice it to say here that owls had such an effect on the Jewish soul and spirit that in one short passage Isaiah had three names for very different owls.

Today nine species are recorded as nesting in Israel: Barn Owl, Scops Owl, Eagle Owl, Brown Fish Owl, Little Owl, Tawny Owl, Hume's Owl, Long-eared Owl and Short-eared Owl. The last two and the Striated Scops Owl are seen on migration too. The largest is the Eagle Owl, whose deep, sonorous, booming call – *oo-hu, oo-hu*, the second syllable falling in pitch – is audible at up to 4 km (2½ miles) away. The smallest is the Scops Owl, closely followed by the Little Owl that became the symbol of Athene, the Greek goddess of wisdom. Both these town dwellers are the commonest owls in Israel today. Their calls could invoke fear in nervous people: the Little Owl at night mewing like a cat, the Scops Owl calling with metronomic precision a short, whistled note, every 2–3 seconds, sometimes for minutes on end at dusk. The Prophet Zephaniah foretold God's destruction of Nineveh in Assyria, saying:

 ZEPHANIAH
CH. 2, V. 14

The desert owl and the screech owl
will roost in her columns.
Their calls will echo through the windows....

The Screech Owl is an old country name in Britain – sometimes still used – for the Barn Owl which is quite a common resident in central and northern Israel. Its call is an unearthly, ghostly screech. The "desert owl" or "horned owl" is most likely the Eagle Owl that is a scarce to uncommon resident in the desert areas of Israel and Sinai. It has two noticeable tufts of feathers on its head, which stand up and look like ears or short horns. As with all owls, its real ears are hidden under the feathers of its head just behind its eyes. The tufts of feathers can be raised and lowered, making the bird's display more or less aggressive or frightening.

The other hawks, buzzards and falcons are only rarely referred to. Job in Chapter 28 writes a poem, trying to answer the question "Where can wisdom be found?" He makes several suggestions and then he writes:

No bird of prey knows that hidden path,
no falcon's eye has seen it.

Falcons have wonderful eyesight, and it is said that wisdom is so difficult to find that even a falcon's eyesight cannot find it. There are eleven species of falcon on the Israeli list. The commonest is the Kestrel, which is a familiar sight in Britain too. Perhaps the most impressive falcon to watch is the Peregrine, specialist hunter of pigeons. As it dives to make a kill it has been timed at over 160 km per hour (100 miles an hour), making it one of the fastest, if not the fastest, bird on Earth. It has decreased in modern times in Israel, as it has in many countries, because of pesticides. It used to nest on Mount Carmel until the 1950s. Now it is quite common on passage. I like to think that it was this falcon that so impressed Job.

LANNER FALCON, SCARCE RESIDENT

The Osprey is a surprise inclusion, if it is correctly identified. It is almost completely a fish eater, spectacularly diving to capture a fish with its outstretched talons. Yet, the Law clearly states that "of all the creatures living in the water of the seas and the streams, you may eat any that have fins and scales". Fish are not unclean. So the Osprey seems to be listed with the other flesh eaters simply because it does eat blood, the life of the fish. Only a few nest in Israel, and it is scarce on passage now.

The other birds specially referred to in the Leviticus list are not birds of prey: the cormorant (Chapter 2), the gull, the stork, the Raven, any kind of heron and the Hoopoe.

Israel's long coastline, the River Jordan Valley, the many fishponds and the Sea of Galilee are all excellent habitats in which to see a cormorant or a member of the gull family. Fourteen species of gulls are on the present Israeli list. Most of them are uncommon or rare, but the Black-headed, Herring and Lesser Black-backed Gulls are frequently seen on passage and as winter visitors now, and would surely have been so two thousand or more years ago. They scavenge at rubbish heaps and catch live food too. All three will flock to follow a plough that is turning up invertebrates in the soil, or will follow a ship, especially a fishing boat, to pick up scraps. Those habits were bound to label them "unclean". Today, the Great Cormorant is an uncommon winter visitor and it is much more likely that the Israelites knew the Pygmy Cormorant. It is now an occasional winter visitor, but formerly it was common, and used to breed at Lake Hula. It was exterminated by fishermen by the mid-1950s and disappeared from the Hula area when the lake and swamps in Turkey were drained.

The stork is undoubtedly the White Stork, which still is a common migrant, passing through the Holy Land in flocks of hundreds, and sometimes thousands, in spring and autumn. A few do breed here. Storks eat unclean food, such as lizards, locusts and other creatures that are detestable because they "move about on the ground" (Leviticus, ch. 11, v. 41). White Storks are large, very obvious birds as they stalk marshes and fields. More people, other than the prophet Jeremiah, certainly would have been deeply impressed by seeing the birds year after year:

> JEREMIAH *Even the stork in the sky*
> CH. 8, V. 7 *knows her appointed seasons.*

Herons feed in a similar way and eat similar food. The heron family includes the bitterns and egrets. They nest in colonies and several are common on passage in spring and autumn, and others are fairly common or common residents. The commonest now is the Little Egret, which is abundant in several areas. It is easily seen; it feeds in cultivated regions, where it

White Stork

preys on "unclean" insects, frogs and small fish. The next most common heron is the Cattle Egret, which did not nest in Israel until the early 1950s, although it used to be a common winter visitor before that. It feeds on "unclean" creatures too, those that are disturbed by the farm animals, as its name implies. The Squacco Heron is another small member of the heron

RAVEN

| BIRDS OF THE BIBLE

family; it is mainly a common passage migrant with
hundreds passing through in March-April
and September especially, stopping
to feed in the wetlands. It was
not recorded breeding in
Israel until 1959.

The Hoopoe is a very
unexpected addition to the list.
It is a gorgeous bird to look at, was featured
on ancient Egyptian murals, and attracts
admiration from tourists and birdwatchers
alike, but presumably was unclean because it
probed in soft ground for worms or similar "detestable creatures". It is a regular, common
migrant through Israel, and is also quite a common breeding bird.

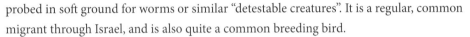

The Raven, the all black, largest of the crows, is known around the world as the Bird of
Doom. In many countries it is associated with death, either because its harsh call in wild,
desolate places foretells it, or because it is seen feeding on corpses. It is listed in various
translations as "every kind of Raven" or "the Raven after its kind". It is clearly an unclean
bird, feeding on carrion, insects, reptiles and worms, indeed almost anything edible. The
way the lawmakers wrote about it is accurate. In Israel, there are, in fact, three species: the
Common Raven, which is widespread across the Northern Hemisphere but is the rarest of
the three in Israel; the Brown-necked Raven, which is a common resident in desert areas;
and the smallest, the Fan-tailed Raven, which is quite common in the Dead Sea region,
south to Eilat and Sinai in mountainous desert areas. One spring I watched two of the Fan-
taileds displaying over Masada by the Dead Sea, diving and twisting in a splendid series of
aerobatic movements, showing clearly their distinctive heavy-billed, short-tailed silhouette.
The writer of Proverbs described the Raven's unclean behaviour well:

 PROVERBS
CH. 30, V. 17

The eye that mocks a father,
that scorns obedience to a mother,
will be pecked out by the ravens of the valley

Intriguingly, the Ravens in other references were not unclean, a detail we shall investigate
further in Chapter 5.

CHAPTER IV

BIRDS FOR FOOD

Many people know that "God gave Solomon wisdom and very great insight, and a breadth of understanding as measureless as the sand on the seashore" (1 Kings, ch. 4, v. 29). We are equally familiar with the account of the building of the Great Temple in Jerusalem, a task that took seven years. The wisdom and riches of Solomon were widely known, as the visit of the Queen of Sheba testifies. What is perhaps not so well known is the fact that Solomon used much of his wealth to feed his entire household, his servants, court officials and their families. The daily provisioning of all these people was a huge task for his district officers. They had to be sure of having at hand, every day:

1 KINGS
CH. 4, VV. 22-23

thirty cors [about 5,000 litres/1,320 gallons] of fine flower and sixty cors [about 10,000 litres/ 2,640 gallons] of meal, ten head of stall-fed cattle, twenty of pasture-fed cattle and a hundred sheep and goats, as well as deer, gazelles, roebucks and choice fowl.

RED JUNGLEFOWL

It is only natural to assume that if Leviticus had given us a list of birds not to eat, then we should be able to find a list of birds which are good for the table, and that it would be fairly straightforward to know exactly which species of "choice fowl" Solomon ate. However, to learn what birds might have been on the menu in biblical times is even more of a detective story than the investigation of the birds' identities covered iin Chapters 2 and 3.

We are not sure what these "choice fowl" were (or "plump fowl" as the Good News Bible calls them). We are so used to a wide choice of "fowls" when we visit a butcher, poulterer or supermarket – chicken, duck, goose, turkey, pheasant – that it is hard to imagine a time without them.

Historians and scientists are reasonably sure that our "chicken" is descended from the Red Junglefowl of the forests of Southeast Asia. The early Indus Valley civilization in India had certainly domesticated them by about 2500 BC. By 1500 BC, it is believed that this valuable

RED JUNGLEFOWL

bird had spread north into China, and as far west as Egypt via tribute paid by Babylon to Pharaoh Thutmose the Third. Solomon reigned in Palestine from 970–930 BC, thus, what we know as the "chicken", could have been on Solomon's table, because when the Queen of Sheba saw "the food on his table ... she was overwhelmed" (1 Kings, ch. 10, v. 5), which suggests his menu was sumptuous and rare. It is well known from written evidence and wall paintings that the Egyptians trapped geese and fattened them. Solomon may have followed their example. In some commentaries there is what seems to me a rather curious interpretation of the Hebrew word "barburim" used for "fowl"; they say that the "choice fowls" were Cuckoos, whose characteristic call is said to be imitated in the Hebrew word. Cuckoos were an ancient delicacy. They are migrants through Palestine, from Europe and south-west Asia, on their way to and from southern Africa. Solomon's district officers could not possibly have provided them as part of the king's *daily* provisions. A more realistic alternative would be that the birds were Guinea Fowl. They are widespread today in the savannahs of Africa, south of the Sahara. However, the birds' domestication was well known in ancient Greece, and the Romans carried on the practice; a Roman mosaic in Cyprus clearly shows a Helmeted Guinea Fowl, the same, white-spotted, grey bird we sometimes see today noisily wandering around a farmyard. The species probably had a more northerly distribution in ancient times when the Sahara was not so expansive and could well have become a favoured dish of the rich, even in Israel.

RED-BREASTED GEESE, FROM AN EGYPTIAN TOMB PAINTING, C. 2600 BC

COMMON QUAIL

Some of the difficulty in deciding what birds were eaten lies in the fact that ordinary people did not eat as much meat as we do, and when they did it was probably a sheep or goat that was part of a religious sacrificial meal. Much of their diet was bread and unleavened cakes, baked daily, vegetables such as "cucumbers, melons, leeks, onions and garlic" (Numbers, ch. 11, v. 5); and fruits, especially grapes, olives and citrus fruits.

Nehemiah began serving King Artaxerxes the First in about 445 BC. Even though he was an exiled Jew, he held a high position of trust as governor of Judah, and eventually persuaded the king to allow him to return to Jerusalem to organize the rebuilding of the city's walls. Nehemiah records that, unlike his predecessors, he did not inflict a heavy tax on the people. "Furthermore," he writes, "a hundred and fifty Jews and officials ate at my table, as well as those who came to us from the surrounding nations. Each day one ox, six choice sheep and

GUINEA FOWL

some poultry were prepared for me" (Nehemiah, ch. 5, v. 17). Interestingly, the *NIV Study Bible* cross references this verse to the verse in 1 Kings which details Solomon's provisions, but Nehemiah uses a different word to name his birds – he writes the Hebrew word "tsippor" instead of "barburim". Clearly, Nehemiah's fare was much less lavish than Solomon's, and was

different enough that another word had to be used. If the birds at Solomon's table were indeed luxurious, such as fattened geese or ducks – Egyptian style – then Nehemiah's fowls could be sensibly translated as "poultry".

The Israelites did trap birds, almost certainly ground-feeding species such as pigeons and doves, partridges and Quails. There are several references to nets and snares being used in these quotations, mostly to illustrate how easily a wicked or careless person could be caught. But all the writers, not just the first one whose statement is a fine example of common sense, must also have written from experience to have created such vivid images:

PROVERBS
CH. 1, V. 17

How useless to spread a net
in full view of the birds!

PROVERBS
CH. 6, V.5

Free yourself like a bird from the snare of the fowler

PROVERBS
CH. 7, V. 23

All at once he followed her...
like a bird darting into a snare

JEREMIAH
CH. 5, V. 26

for among my people there are wicked men
who lay snares like a fowler's net

AMOS
CH. 3, V. 5

Does a bird fall into a trap on the ground
if the striker is not set for it?

The last one seems to refer to what we call a "clap net". It is still used by bird catchers and ornithologists who are interested in migration studies and need to fit a small identity ring on the birds' legs. This net was popular in Egypt, and probably in Palestine too. It would be laid on the ground, covering an area of 8 sq. m (80 sq. ft) or more, and would be closed through 180° at a given signal by pulling on a rope. All three kinds of birds mentioned above are attracted to seed and the ideal catching site was probably a natural or artificial food source.

In Israel, during biblical times, the common wild pigeons likely to be seen in flocks were the Rock Dove (the ancestor of our feral town pigeons), Stock Dove, Wood Pigeon and Turtle Dove. In Canon Tristram's time, and no doubt centuries before, the gregarious Rock Dove

TURTLE DOVE

could be seen in thousands in Jericho, in hundreds near Hebron, and "words cannot convey an impression of the multitude" in the region of Nahal Amud. Today, it is much less common. The Stock Dove and Wood Pigeon are mostly winter visitors to Palestine and their numbers vary from a few in some years to many in others and sometimes in flocks of hundreds – just what the Israelite fowlers would have prayed for.

Two other doves are common in Israel today. The Collared Dove's original range was India and across Central Africa. It may have been introduced in historical times to the Middle East; in the 1940s, for example, it bred only in the Bet She'an valley and the southern coastal plain. The Palm or Laughing Dove was definitely introduced from Africa by the Muslims to their mosques, so it could not have been earlier than about AD 700 (the Dome of the Rock on the Temple Mount was not built by the Muslims until 688-691). Although these two small, confiding, town-dwelling doves are commonly seen today by visitors and pilgrims, they would not have been hunted by the Israelites.

It is a very different story with regard to the migratory Turtle Dove, which is, and so far as we know always has been, a common summer visitor: in April I have seen some 200 gather in about three minutes on telegraph wires along the road in the Jordan Valley, and have heard many from Jerusalem to Caesarea Philippi repeating their purring song:

SONG OF SOLOMON
CH. 2, V. 12

The voice of the Turtle Dove is heard in the land.

The doves and pigeons would have been good to catch and eat, though only the latter is specifically named.

Four members of the pheasant family are still popular game birds and would certainly have attracted the attention of Palestinian fowlers and egg collectors; they are the Chukar and Sand Partridges, the Black Francolin and the Quail. The first is the most common today in fruit groves, fields and open ground. The second is locally common in the Jordan Valley in rocky places south of the Sea of Galilee as far as the Negev. The Francolin is a bird of dense vegetation, farmed or wild, in the Jordan Valley. The migratory Quail passes through in spring and autumn in great numbers, and many stay to breed. It is a small bird, only 16–18 cm (6–7 in) long, and is easily hidden in the pastures or wild grasslands that it favours. Partridges are not very vocal but the Quail's three-note call gives it away: *wet-my-lips, wet-my-lips*. There are two stories in the Old Testament that retell the miraculous arrival of many Quails, just when the Israelites were moaning to Moses: "If only we had meat to eat!" The first is in Exodus, chapter 16 (see page 53), and the second in Numbers, chapter 11. This may seem an extraordinary, even impossible, occurrence. However, the Quail is the only migrant member of the pheasant family which breeds in Europe and the Middle East; it migrates south to spend the winter south of the Sahara, and even today, in some years, it is extremely abundant along the Mediterranean coast. In times past it has been known to arrive in flocks of several thousands in some areas. It is still a much sought-after bird for food, and flocks now are more likely to be numbered in the tens. As recently as between 1920 and 1930, during the autumn migration, the Egyptians were known to have trapped up to a million annually. The Israelites in the Wilderness certainly did enjoy a huge feast of Quails!

There is a very revealing hunting reference to be found in a conversation that young David had with King Saul. David was a fugitive from Saul's jealous anger, and had the chance to kill him but

SAND
PARTRIDGE

refused, for as he said: "Who can lay a hand on the Lord's anointed and be guiltless?". (1 Samuel, ch. 26, v. 9) David shouted to Saul's guard and Saul heard him and called out to him. David asked why Saul was chasing him, and what was he guilty of. He ended by saying: "The king of Israel has come out to look for a flea - as one hunts a partridge in the mountain" (1 Samuel, ch. 26, v. 20). David was suggesting that the king was making a fool of himself in his fanatical pursuit of an innocent man. His figure of speech suggests a big hunting party out to catch a very small meal. The most likely partridge that David had in mind is the Sand Partridge that is resident in the wild country in the Dead Sea depression that David was in.

CHUKAR

The species is still called "qore" in Hebrew today, the very word used in the Old Testament stories. Both species are hunted for food and sport to this day.

The Prophet Jeremiah is the only other writer who names the partridge, in a rather strange proverb:

⬱ JEREMIAH
CH. 17, V. 11

Like a partridge that hatches eggs it did not lay
is the man who gains riches by unjust means. ⬱

Partridges are actually very good parents, unlike the closely related Pheasant, and do not steal other birds' eggs, or lay eggs in others' nests as Cuckoos do. The proverb is based on an ancient belief that a hen partridge did steal eggs and put them in her own nest – how else could one account for such a large clutch? Ornithologists today have studied partridges and know that a Chukar will commonly lay 8–15 eggs and up to 20 is not unknown; Canon Tristram discovered a nest with 26. The Chukar is common to very common throughout Israel today; it is found in fields, orchards, groves and all kinds of open ground. It is a very good candidate for the bird to which Jeremiah was referring.

Other references do not name a species, but do suggest that the Israelites were very aware of game birds' nests and took their eggs for food. Through the words of the prophet, God describes how he will defeat Assyria:

ISAIAH
CH. 10, VV. 13-14

I plundered their treasures...
As one reaches into a nest
So my hand reached for the wealth of nations,
as men gather abandoned eggs,
so I gathered all the countries;
not one flapped a wing,
or opened its mouth to chirp.

Later the same prophet describes how the nation of Moab that had so often oppressed Israel would suffer:

ISAIAH
CH. 16, V. 2

Like fluttering birds
pushed from the nest,
So are the women of Moab
at the fords of the Arnon.

I am sure the young Israelites, maybe even Isaiah himself, had been out bird-nesting to collect partridge or Quail eggs to eat. Nowadays we simply pick a box from the supermarket shelf! Perhaps our reading of the Israelites' close relationship with the land should make us shamefully aware of how easily we take our rich fare for granted, and how rarely we really understand what we are saying when we repeat, "Give us this day our daily bread".

The *Checklist* records that the local people in Sinai still catch Quails with nets. Of all the game birds this is the only one that is the subject of a famous story in the Old Testament. The Israelites had left Egypt and were on their long journey back to Palestine. In the second month after they had left Egypt they grumbled:

EXODUS
CH. 16, VV. 3 & 11-13

"If only we had died by the Lord's hand in Egypt!
There we sat round pots of meat and ate all the
food we wanted, but you [Moses] have brought us
out into this desert to starve this entire assembly to
death."...The Lord said to Moses, "I have heard the
grumbling of the Israelites. Tell them, 'At twilight
you will eat meat...'" That evening Quail came and
covered the camp.

The story is elaborated in the book of Numbers:

Now the wind went out from the Lord and drove

Quail in from the sea. It brought them down all

around the camp to about three feet above the

ground, as far as a day's walk in any direction.

All that day and night and all the next day the

people went out and gathered Quail. No-one

gathered less than ten homers (i.e. probably about

60 bushels/ 2,200 litres).

NUMBERS
CH. 11, vv. 31-32

The Psalmist many years later exhorted the Israelites to remember all of God's goodness to them and to worship Him. One of the things he reminds them of is the escape from Egypt:

PSALM
105, vv. 37-40

He brought out Israel, laden with silver and gold,

and from among their tribes no-one faltered.

Egypt was glad when they left,

Because dread of Israel had fallen on them.

He spread out a cloud as a covering,

and a fire to give light at night.

They asked, and he brought them Quail

and satisfied them with the bread of heaven.

Thus refreshed and fed with Quails (and manna too, which is believed to be a kind of honeydew), one would have thought the Israelites would have been grateful, but soon lack of water upset them further and resulted in more ingratitude and disobedience. It was forty years before they were ready to enter the Promised Land. We would do well to remember God's blessings to us, and say as the Psalmist did at the beginning of this same psalm:

Give thanks to the Lord, call on his name;

make known among the nations what he has done.

Sing to him, sing praise to him;

tell all his wonderful acts...

....Praise the Lord.

It is clear from the Old Testament writers that the Israelites did not shop for eggs or fowl as we do, nor did they simply wait for birds to fall from heaven. They were active hunters. The prophets knew this well and mention snares, traps and nets in their descriptions of the ways that God eventually punished wicked men and nations (see also page 49). Amos spoke the word of the Lord to Israel in the eighth century BC. His uncompromising criticism of Israel's sinfulness and the fact that she would suffer were figuratively described thus:

AMOS
CH. 3, V. 5

*Does a bird fall into a trap on the ground
where no snare has been set?
Does a trap spring up from the earth
when there is nothing to catch?*

One of the most detailed accounts of a fowler at work is Hosea's description of how the Israelites would be taught a lesson by God for their wickedness; he was writing in the middle of the eighth century BC:

PIN-TAILED (LEFT) AND BLACK-BELLIED SANDGROUSE

Wood Pigeon: adult above, juvenile below

Ephraim is like a dove,
easily deceived and senseless -
no calling to Egypt,

≈ HOSEA

CH. 7, V. 11-13

no turning to Assyria.
When they go I will throw my net over them;
I will pull them down like birds of the air.
When I hear them flocking together,
I will catch them. ≈

Ephraim was Joseph's son, and by Hosea's time the name stood for Israel. Nets were obviously an effective and well-known way of catching birds, such as sandgrouse, which are relatives of doves and which had come down to a pool to drink, as was their habit. Bildad, one of Job's so-called Comforters, adds to the prophet's description when he is explaining to Job what happens to a wicked man who has been found out – he will feel like a bird or an animal that has been trapped:

His feet thrust him into a net
and he wanders into its mesh.

≈ JOB

CH. 18, VV. 8-10

A trap seizes him by the heel;
a snare holds him fast.
A noose is hidden for him on the ground;
a trap lies in his path. ≈

The final word from the Old Testament writers on the subject of birds for food is not so much about what they ate, but contains a message for us all:

Contend, O Lord, with those who contend with me....
....Since they hid their net for me without cause

≈ PSALM

35, VV. 7-8

and without cause dug a pit for me,
may ruin overtake them by surprise -
may the net they hid entangle them.... ≈

We should be careful, not so much as to desire revenge on those who quarrel with us, but to ensure that the things we do and say which might upset others, do not get us entangled as well.

CHAPTER V

BIRDS AND PARTICULAR PEOPLE

n the previous chapter we read about two Old Testament characters who were particularly thankful to birds for food – Moses and Solomon. Here we will read about Noah, Abraham and Elijah.

One of the very first stories in the Bible speaks of many birds. Noah took into the Ark "seven of every kind of bird...every bird according to its kind" (Genesis, ch. 8, vv. 3 & 14). Whether you believe literally that Noah's Ark could carry seven of each of the world's 10,000 species (that is the present estimate, not counting any that have become extinct in the meantime), or whether you understand the story to be a figurative way of describing a huge natural disaster, the fact remains there was a great flood in prehistoric times. It has been recorded in the twelve tablets of the *Gilgamesh Epic* from the Sumerian and Babylonian civilizations of Mesopotamia, between the rivers Tigris and Euphrates. Genesis was probably written as early as 1300 BC. The story of the Flood in the *Gilgamesh Epic* is many years earlier than Genesis, from c.1600 BC. The names in the two accounts differ, but both the stories are so similar that scholars generally believe that the biblical Flood story was borrowed from the earlier one.

The Bible records that "every living thing on the face of the earth was wiped out", but later it was discovered that many species had survived. To Noah it would have appeared that the whole world had been flooded – to him and his contemporaries the world was Mesopotamia and nearby. There is a clue in the story that explains why species were later found to have survived. The popular song about Noah's Ark declares that: "The animals came in two by two". But Noah took *seven* birds of every species, male and female, so that at least two would reproduce "to keep their various kinds alive throughout the earth". The other five would be needed as food and as burnt offerings in the sacrifices Noah would make (Chapter 11). Only two of the "unclean" creatures were kept because Mankind had no special use for them.

The turning point in Noah's ordeal in the Ark comes when he uses two particular birds on reconnaissance missions. He sends out a Raven and a dove to try to find land:

After forty days Noah opened the window he had
made in the ark and sent out a Raven, and it kept

RAVEN

GENESIS

CH. 8, VV. 6-12

flying back and forth until the water had dried up from the earth. Then he sent out a dove to see if the water had receded from the surface of the ground. But the dove could find no place to set its feet because there was water over all the surface of the earth; so it returned to Noah in the ark. He reached out his hand and took the dove and brought it back to himself in the ark. He waited seven more days and again sent out the dove from the ark. When the dove returned to him in the evening, there in its beak was a freshly picked olive leaf! Then Noah knew that the water had receded from the earth. He waited seven more days and sent the dove out again, but this time it did not return to him.

The Raven is an interesting choice. It is usually thought of in European folklore – and even further afield – as being the Bird of Doom (see also page 43). This was well known in the 17th century in Shakespeare's time. In his play *Macbeth,* Lady Macbeth declares that the Raven "croaks the fatal entrance of Duncan" (Duncan the king, who is later murdered by Macbeth). It is not so well known that the Raven has an ambivalent character. It is a supernatural bird, sometimes good, sometimes evil. Scholars believe this ambivalence can be traced historically to two traditions, Judaism and Christianity (the good), and heathen (the bad). Whichever way people saw the Raven they believed it was a supernatural bird. So, when it flew "back and forth" on its release it appears, on our first reading of this, that it did not return to Noah in the Ark and so it perished at sea. However, as a supernatural creature Noah would have believed it had miraculously survived, and that augured well for him.

The dove's release and its return hints at the fact that early man was already familiar with breeding doves that came back to the dovecote or loft. Doves and pigeons are much studied today by scientists who are interested in their homing instincts. Pigeon fanciers today rely on the birds' ability to return home after long journeys of hundreds of miles. Thus it should not be surprising for us to realize that Noah had high hopes that his dove would return.

It was most likely that his dove was a Rock Dove (see page 49), which is sometimes called Rock Pigeon, and is the species from which our feral and homing pigeons are descended. When it did return with a sprig of olive leaves it was a sure sign that the Flood was subsiding. The

ROCK DOVE

likelihood of Noah having a "homing pigeon" is certain. We know that Neolithic man of the Later Stone Age engaged in primitive crop growing and stock rearing. That was in about 9,000–6,000 BC in south-west Asia, and later, 4,000–2,400 BC in Europe. Rock Doves need cliff crevices or ledges in caves for nest sites, so it is quite possible that the first close contact that man had with these birds was when they nested in his home. It would not have been difficult for him to raise some squabs and discover that they became dependent on him for their care. The story of the Flood is well within this time scale. Archaeology in Mesopotamia has revealed evidence of several floods between c.4,000 and c.2,500 BC. We can be quite confident that Noah's dove was very like the one the Sumerians kept at this time for food and sacrifice. The image of the dove and its leaves became the source for the ancient and widely known symbol of peace.

Later in Genesis we read of God's call to Abram to lead the people, and about Abram's great covenant with God that ended with Abram (which means "exalted father") being renamed by God, Abraham ("father of many"). Part of Abraham's response to God was his preparing a holy sacrifice as commanded by God:

≫ GENESIS
CH. 15, V. 9

So the lord said to him, "Bring me a heifer, a goat and a ram, each three years old, along with a dove and a young pigeon." ≫

The New English Bible deliberately translates the dove as a Turtle Dove, a very common migrant through and breeder in the Middle East. It would have been hunted in Abraham's time in spring and autumn (see page 50). It is a really suitable translation as contemporary Hebrew records "tor mazuy" as the Turtle Dove's name in bird books today. In the original Hebrew in Genesis it is "tor". Doves and vultures – what a wonderful mix of Creation there was in Abraham's time! For that is exactly what we find when we read on beyond the reference to his sacrificial dove:

 GENESIS
CH. 15, vv. 10-11

Abram brought all these to [the Lord], cut them in two and arranged the halves opposite each other; the birds, however, he did not cut in half. Then birds of prey came down on the carcasses, but Abram drove them away. ⤳

That birds of prey came down on the carcasses is not surprising. It is exactly what vultures do today, and they were much more common in Abraham's day. In Africa and Asia today, there is grave concern at the declining populations of several species, the result of the birds being poisoned by feeding on dead cows that had been given chemical treatments by vets to prevent bovine diseases. As recently as forty years ago, in countries where vultures were common, dozens would gather at a carcass and hundreds would collect at village and town rubbish dumps. Now they are rare.

The Living Bible and the popular Good News Bible, both translate the "birds of prey" of this passage as "vultures". Five species of vulture have been recorded in Israel. Abraham almost certainly knew the Egyptian and the Griffon Vultures, which have always been the commonest since they were first properly studied two centuries ago. Both are carrion eaters. The former is (and probably was in Abraham's time) a "prominent eater of refuse and may be seen on kitchen refuse together with kites and ravens" (*The Birds of Israel* by Uzi Paz, 1987). The Griffon Vulture is one of the largest raptors in the world; its grey-brown bulk dwarfs the slimmer black and white Egyptian. In subtropical and tropical lands, vultures through the ages have done mankind a great service by getting rid of carrion. Griffons in particular are communal birds, and as soon as they learned that there was food at a human camp or sacrificial altar, they would have gathered in a threatening flock waiting for a chance to feed on the offal thrown aside. It is not surprising that Abraham felt he had to drive them away. He had a two-fold reason for doing this: his worship was not over and the vultures were "unclean". So Abraham guarded his sacrifice, and it was only when the sun had set that

Vulture

A Hoopoe's nest is usually inside the hole

God made His covenant with Abraham and promised: "To your descendants I give this land". The seemingly strange action of cutting the animals in half is part of the detailed instructions for the conduct of a sacrifice recorded in Leviticus (this is dealt with in more detail in Chapter 11, *Birds and Worship*).

King Solomon is remembered in the Bible not only as a man with great wisdom but also as one with a great knowledge of God's creatures:

> ⋙ 1 KINGS
> CH. 4, V. 33
>
> *He spoke of trees and plants, from the Lebanon cedars to the hyssop that grows on walls; he talked about animals, birds, reptiles, and fish.* ⋙

Legend has it that one day when on his travels, a Hoopoe flew over the king and sheltered him from the sun. Solomon was so pleased that he rewarded the bird with a golden crown, but the bird returned later explaining that it was so miserable because everyone kept trying to steal the crown. The compassionate king gave the bird a spectacular crest instead, which the Hoopoe still wears to this day!

A hundred or so years after Solomon, Ahab was king of Israel, the northern kingdom in the Holy Land. He ruled for twenty-two years till his death in 853 BC, during which time the Israelites, urged on by Queen Jezebel, increasingly worshipped Baal. The king "did more evil in the eyes of the Lord than any of those before him" (1 Kings, ch. 16, v. 30). Elijah the prophet, whose name means "The Lord is my God", spoke out against the sinful nation and prophesied that there would be a drought with no dew or rain for the next few years, as a divine punishment. Clearly this put Elijah in great danger, especially when we learn later that Jezebel persecuted the Hebrew prophets, so he fled:

GRIFFON VULTURE

Then the word of the Lord came to Elijah: "Leave here, turn eastward and hide in the Kerith Ravine, east of the Jordan. You will drink from the brook, and I have ordered the ravens to feed you." So he did what the Lord had told him. He went to the Kerith Ravine, east of the Jordan, and stayed there. The ravens brought him bread and meat in the morning and bread and meat in the evening, and he drank from the brook.

1 KINGS
CH. 17, VV. 2-6

STOCK DOVE

Noah was served by a Raven, and even more miraculously so was Elijah. Ravens are omnivorous. A pair defends a territory all year round, and the jet-black birds, with their resonant, deep, croaking calls are a familiar sight in wild places right across the Northern Hemisphere, even in a desert such as the Kerith Valley to which Elijah had fled. The location of Kerith is uncertain. It is thought that it might be the gorge of a tributary of the River Yarmuk that flows into the Jordan south of Galilee. Ravens nest on cliff ledges, or sometimes in a tree. Elijah would not have disturbed a nesting pair as he hid from Ahab. I like to think his food was a sharing of what the Ravens brought to their chicks in a nest. A desperate person, hiding in a desert valley, but by a stream, would be very happy to eat whatever a Raven brought.

There are actually three species of raven in Israel: the Common Raven (the biggest and the one with the wide distribution already mentioned), the Brown-necked and the Fan-tailed Raven. The last two are actually most at home in desert habitats. I have vivid memories of watching the aerobatic flight of Fan-tailed Ravens at Masada and Qumran near the Dead Sea. I am sure that Elijah would have been equally thrilled by these large birds, all splendid fliers and noted for their flight displays. He would have been thrilled, I believe, even though "the raven after its kind" is on the list of unclean food (Chapter 3). He would soon have understood that what they provided was not unclean even though their own flesh might be considered so. Elijah would have increasingly realized that God the Creator was in charge, not the Law. As he hid by the Kerith Ravine he may well have thought of the proverb:

 PROVERBS
CH. 30, V. 17

The eye that mocks a father, that scorns obedience to a mother, will be pecked out by the Ravens of the valley, will be eaten by the vultures.

That portrays the widely believed *evil* side of the Raven's character, but although Elijah had observed Israel's great disobedience and would have felt fearful when he first saw the Ravens, his own trust in God would have helped him overcome his fear and revulsion. He had to think differently, just as Peter did many centuries later, when he had to overcome his revulsion at what he thought was unclean and believe that what God was showing him was good. Elijah and Peter did change, and believed, as many people do today, God's word to Peter: "Do not call anything impure that God has made clean"(Acts of the Apostles, ch. 10, v. 15).

CHAPTER VI

JOB'S BIRDS

Many people traditionally think of Job only as a man who suffered dreadfully. The three men, known as "Job's Comforters", attempted to soothe his sorrow and despair at the death of his entire family, but they did not really help at all. Their nickname lives on in the English language as the name we give to people who think they are comforting but who actually just increase the misery. However, a careful reading of Job reveals the story to be much more complex than that.

We are well used to reading detailed, well-illustrated books about natural history, and watching amazing television films on creatures from all around the world. The readers of Job would have felt the same sense of wonder when they read the last part of this book in particular.

The anonymous author is believed to have written some time between the seventh and second centuries BC, certainly in the Iron Age becasue there is a mention of the metal in chapter 19, verse 24. Iron did not come into common use in the Near East till about the 12th century BC. Then Man lived close to Nature but did not study it scientifically as is done today by scientists and experts such as Sir David Attenborough, the television filmmaker, and Stephen Jay Gould and Richard Fitter, both distinguished authors of many natural history books. Job and his contemporaries saw the practical use of wood, iron and stone, enjoyed the fruits of the earth and fed on the meat of the animals they herded. To them these were evidence of God's creative power and majesty. That was well recorded in song in their Psalms which hark back at least to King David's time (1010–970 BC), or maybe earlier:

 PSALM
50, vv. 1 & 10-11

The mighty one, God, the Lord,
speaks and summons the earth
from the rising of the sun to the place where it sets...
...every animal of the forest is mine,
and the cattle on a thousand hills.
I know every bird in the mountains,
and the creatures of the field are mine

All of Creation is there, not just wildlife and naturalists.

The considerable number of examples of God's Creation that are mentioned in Job has led many readers to declare that the author is the finest naturalist in the Old Testament. He and his contemporaries, and the Israelites later, carefully observed the world around them and wrote about it (and no doubt talked about it at length too, if the amount that Job's Comforters had to say is anything to go by). They wrote (and spoke) in ways that illustrated how they felt

Buzzard

about the world and their own lives. Of such is Job's first reference to a bird, or rather something associated with a bird:

PEREGRINE

If only my anguish could be weighed
and all my misery be placed on the scales!
It would surely outweigh the sand on the seas -
no wonder my words have been impetuous.
The arrows of the Almighty are in me,
my spirit drinks in their poison;
God's terrors are marshalled against me.
Does a wild donkey bray when it has grass,
or an ox bellow when it has fodder?
Is tasteless food eaten without salt,
or is there flavour in the white of an egg?
I refuse to touch it;
such food makes me ill.

JOB
CH. 6, VV. 2-7

Job's Comforter, Eliphaz, argues that Job is suffering after the violent death of his sons and daughters because he cannot be wholly innocent from sin, so this is a punishment from God. However, even as a donkey brays when it has no food, Job believes he has the right to shout because he has nothing, neither has he had any helpful words of comfort from his friends so that is as tasteless as the egg. Later he acknowledges that his real suffering is because he cannot find God who could be able to help him:

JOB
CH. 23, VV.3-4

If only I knew where to find him;
if only I could go to his dwelling!
I would state my case before him
and fill my mouth with arguments.
I would find out what he would answer me,
and consider what he would say.

But it was a long time before Job heard from God. Till then Job speaks eloquently about his troubled state of mind. He feels that the scales of Justice are weighed against him and God "mocks the despair of the innocent".

He goes on in a frame of mind that clearly shows his despair:

> ◈ JOB
> CH. 9, VV. 25-26
> *My days are swifter than a runner;*
> *they fly away without a glimpse of joy.*
> *They skim past like boats of papyrus,*
> *like eagles swooping down on their prey.* ◈

There is a double-edged point in the eagle image: the speed of the bird of prey is impressive and perfectly illustrates the way Job is thinking about how his life is slipping by; and in a dark, sinister way the eagle represents the cruel justice whose prey is Job.

Later the Comforter called Zophar also talks about Job's sin and his apparent lack of wisdom in arguing with God. Job replies that animals and birds have wisdom, and surely God has provided that:

> ◈ JOB
> CH. 12, V. 7
> *But ask the animals, and they will teach you,*
> *or the birds of the air, they will tell you...* ◈

Many people today feel like that. Charles Darwin, however, agonized over his interpretation of what the lives of animals and birds told him. They showed him Evolution, not instant Creation as the Church taught, but he eventually published his theories in 1859 in his famous book, *The Origin of Species*. Today Richard Dawkins, a professor at Oxford University and an internationally famous evolutionist after his books *The Selfish Gene* (1989) and *The Blind Watchmaker* (1986) were published, says people who believe in God are "deluded" and God is "superfluous" to an understanding of Creation. Job, however, who had been dealt a cruel blow and was poorly served by his three Comforters, went through mental torture as he tried to find an answer to his suffering, but he could still say:

> ◈ JOB
> CH. 12, V. 13
> *...To God belong wisdom and power;*
> *counsel and understanding are his.* ◈

Many people today are still prepared to declare their faith in God as Job did.

Job and his Comforters discuss at length where they may find wisdom, and Job in particular describes how difficult it is to be wise despite his former belief that the wildlife he was familiar with could teach him about it. His despair conquers him.

Man can excavate for treasures, but:

Where does wisdom come from?
~~ JOB   *Where does understanding dwell?*
CH. 28, vv.20-21   *It is hidden from the eyes of every living thing,*
Concealed even from the birds of the air. ~~

He had already explained how man can "tunnel through the rock" and mine sapphires and gold, but cannot find wisdom, and he admits now that:

~~ JOB   *No bird of prey knows that hidden path,*
CH. 28, v.7   *No falcon's eye has seen it.* ~~

It should be humbling for us today to realize that about three thousand years ago a man was so observant of the birds around him that he knew how acute the eyesight of birds of prey was. The eye of a bird has reached a state of perfection found in no other animal, and compared with Man, birds have enormously large eyes which provide larger and sharper images (see *The Life of Birds* by Joel Carl Welty, 1964, and later editions). Birds of prey, such as falcons, unlike many other species, have binocular vision enabling them to focus on prey right in front of them. Careful study has revealed that the Common Buzzard, a widespread hawk in Europe and Asia, and one which Job may have seen, has a visual acuity at least eight times that of Man. Falcons, too, can see prey clearly from a great distance. So if those birds with wonderful eyesight cannot see wisdom, Job is convinced that, despite what he said earlier, he will never find it.

For all his appreciation of the marvel of the eagle's flight and the falcon's sight, Job was ambivalent about his feelings for birds. At the height of his suffering, which was physical as well as mental and spiritual, he feels so desolate that he says:

I have become a brother of jackals,
~~ JOB   *a companion of owls.*
CH. 30, vv. 28, 29   *My skin grows black and peels;*
my body burns with fever.... ~~

The nocturnal habits and weird calls of owls make superstitious men in many countries fearful even today, as happened in Job's time. How often have you watched a film at the cinema or on television and heard how the call of owls increases the night's creepy atmosphere? Job is so depressed that his fear of animals and birds of prey has gone, and he feels he has become part of the nightlife he formerly feared.

Elihu, his friend, valiantly tries to help Job, but he does not have the same closeness to the natural world that Job has:

> *Men cry out under a load of oppression;*
> *they plead for relief from the arm of the powerful.*
>
> *JOB*
> CH. 35, VV. 9-11
>
> *But no-one says, "Where is God my Maker,*
> *who gives songs in the night,*
> *who teaches more to us than to the beasts of the earth*
> *and makes us wiser than the birds of the air?"*

Job's friend does, however, give Job better advice than any of his three Comforters: Eliphaz, Bildad and Zophar. He understands that God loves Mankind and can calm his fears – with the help of those songs in the night. Elihu claims Job is talking nonsense, but he does prepare Job for the arrival of God in a storm:

> *JOB*
> CH. 38, VV. 2, 3
>
> *Who is this that darkens my counsel*
> *with words without knowledge?*
> *Brace yourself like a man;*
> *I will question you,*
> *and you shall answer me.*

SPARROWHAWK

It is God's questioning that gives Job complete faith in God's goodness, and in these questions the author of the book of Job reveals his greatest knowledge of God's Creation. The questions follow thick and fast, asking Job if can he do this or that, is he as strong as this, as fast as that – all the images come from Creation, on land, in the sea, in the air. The importance of the seasons is revealed in one question:

> *JOB*
> CH. 38, V. 36
> GOOD NEWS BIBLE
>
> *Who tells the ibis when the Nile will flood...?*

Other translations admit that several words here are of uncertain meaning and translate the question as, "Who put wisdom into the hearts of men?" or something similar. In Chapter 1 we learn that Job came from the land of Uz that was a large territory to the east of the River Jordan. As a "great man of the east" he may have known about the importance of the Nile's regular flooding to maintain the richness of the bordering farmland. If you have travelled down the Nile as I have, you will be familiar with two species of ibis, the Sacred and the Glossy. The ancient Egyptians believed the former was the manifestation of Thoth, their god of wisdom and writing, which makes us think of the other reconstructions of the verse. Unfortunately this ibis is not known in the Jordan Valley so Job would only have got to know it from travellers' tales. The other species, the Glossy Ibis, is found commonly along the Nile, and less so in Israel (and presumably was there in ancient times too). This is a large bird which Job is more likely to have seen and might, therefore, have helped him understand God's question.

The detailed account of the life of the Ostrich in the book is particularly well known:

The wings of the ostrich flap joyfully,
but they cannot compare with the pinions
and feathers of the stork.
She lays her eggs on the ground
and lets them warm in the sand,
unmindful that a foot may crush them,
that some wild animal may trample them.
She treats her young harshly, as if they were not hers;
she cares not that her labour was in vain
for God did not endow her with wisdom
or give a share of good sense.
Yet when she spreads her feathers to run,
she laughs at horse and rider.

JOB
CH. 39, VV. 13-18

A cock Ostrich is flightless but flaps its white plumes in courtship display and as it runs. Ostriches were hunted in ancient times for these feathers as an ancient Assyrian seal shows; the plumes are still much sought after as part of a lady's finery. Certainly a fine example, which is the opposite of the flightless Ostrich, is the high flying, soaring, migrant White Stork, which migrates through Palestine in spring and autumn in flocks of many hundreds

(Chapter 9). Ostriches today lay their eggs in a simple depression in the ground where they are in danger of being trampled by wild camels or antelopes. Sometimes two hens lay in one nest, for the cock is polygamous, which may explain why the writer believes that the hen does not care for her brood. Modern study of this bird has revealed that the male and female do incubate the eggs, and both care for the chicks.

GLOSSY IBIS

Ostriches used to be widespread in the Middle East, where it was one of six subspecies, the only one outside Africa. It was smaller than the African races, but still looked like the others – the largest birds in the world today. Scientists believe it is one of the most primitive birds now in existence. Perhaps, instinctively, the writer of Job realized this, and that is why he portrays it without wisdom. It used to be found in the Syrian and Arabian deserts; in the Negev and Sinai. The proliferation of firearms after the First World War, and hunting with motor vehicles were its death knell, and it has been extinct there since the 1930s. In 1973, 18 chicks were reintroduced into Israel, at the Hai Bar Nature Reserve, where it was hoped to breed and the young released in the Negev. Unlike the identifications of some birds' names which are in doubt, the Hebrew of the Bible calls the Ostrich "ya-annah" which is very close to the modern "ya-en".

God bombards Job with questions. Can he make rain, ice and dew? Can he make lightning? Can he make grass grow, or hunt prey for a lioness, or does he provide "the raven with its quarry when its fledgling croak for lack of food"? (Job, ch. 38 v. 41, New English Bible). Ravens really do "croak" which the NEB admits is a probable reading; the New International Version is much less descriptive with its "cry out". It is fascinating that the author names the Raven and implies that it is supplied with food by God. Of all the birds he could have chosen, he names an *unclean* species. It seems that Job's author made a deliberate choice to emphasize that God cares for all Creation and has not divided it into "good" and "bad", "clean" and "unclean". Centuries later when Jesus was talking to His disciples, on one occasion He said:

> *Therefore, I tell you, do not worry about your life, what you will eat; or about your body, what you will wear. Life is more than food, and the body more than clothes. Consider the ravens. They do not sow or reap, they have no storeroom or barn; yet God feeds them. And how much more valuable you are than birds.*

ST LUKE
CH. 12, vv. 22-24

Jesus was surely remembering Elijah's and Job's Ravens, and making the same point that *all* God's creatures are equally precious to Him.

Chapter 39 continues with splendid poetry describing "the eagle", as New International Version and New Revised Standard Version call it, but the New English Bible translates the name differently, in line with NIV's footnote alternative:

> *Do you instruct the vulture to fly high and build its nest aloft? It dwells among the rocks and there it lodges; its station is a crevice in the rock; from there it searches for food, keenly scanning the distance, that its brood may be gorged with blood; and where the slain are, there the vulture is.*

JOB
CH. 39, vv. 27 - 30,
NEW ENGLISH BIBLE

Ostrich

The description does fit the behaviour of a vulture perfectly, rather than an eagle as we have already seen. The Griffon Vultures of Palestine still do nest high on cliffs. They do search over great distances for food. Modern studies in Spain have shown that this species may roam over an area with a radius of 50 km (30 miles) from the colony. Sadly, today, this impressive bird has decreased considerably in Israel. In the mid-19th century colonies of more than a hundred pairs were known on Mount Carmel, near Tiberias, the Golan Heights, the Negev and elsewhere. By 1984 only 68 pairs were known in the whole country. The extensive use of agricultural pesticides found as residues in carcasses have poisoned them.

LEVANT SPARROWHAWK

| BIRDS OF THE BIBLE

There are no corpses of the slain after a battle as there used to be in the old days to keep the colonies flourishing. One of the last questions which God asks Job is:

> ✎ JOB
> CH. 39, V. 26
>
> *Does the hawk take flight by your wisdom*
> *and spread his wings towards the south?* ✐

This is one of literature's most ancient references to the migration of birds. Hawks of several species really do migrate through the Middle East from their breeding grounds further north, on their way to winter in Africa. Job's author must have been familiar with the stirring sight of these birds of prey that pass by so regularly in spring and autumn. Any observant person 3,000 years ago would be bound to notice them. They were well worth including in God's list of questions. More detail about these hawks is described in Chapter 9, *The Migration of Birds*.

At the end of the book we must admit that Job had lacked the wisdom, authority, skill and creativity which, as God revealed in his questioning, was needed in Creation. But Job was humble and understanding enough to snap out of his despair and say:

> ✎ JOB
> CH. 40, V. 2
>
> *I am unworthy - how can I reply to you?* ✐

But finally, after God's last speech, Job firmly replies:

> ✎ JOB
> CH. 42, VV. 1-3
>
> *I know then you can do all things;*
> *no plan of yours can be thwarted.*
> *You asked, "Who is this that obscures*
> *my counsel without knowledge?"*
> *Surely I spoke of things I did not understand,*
> *things too wonderful for me to know.* ✐

We may not feel as wretched as Job did and despise ourselves and repent in dust and ashes, but even after all the scientific explanations in books, lectures and films, there are still things which we feel are too wonderful for us to know, and are surely from God. Believing that, we too may find like Job, that "The Lord blessed the latter part of [our lives] more than the first" (Job, ch. 42, v. 12).

CHAPTER VII

BIRDS
AND JESUS

I n these days of global warming, habitat loss and declining populations of once common birds, it would be good to find that Jesus had some definitive message for His believers about Creation and our stewardship of it. Unfortunately that is not so. However, commentators on the teachings of Jesus have, over the years, often written about His considerable ability to preach His gospel with the aid of parables and other illustrations which depend on lively descriptions of the world about Him: farming, animals, flowers – and birds. So, indirectly, He does tell us a great deal about what birds should mean to us.

He could not really have been aware of the first contact He had with birds:

 ST LUKE
CH. 2, vv. 22-24

When the time of their purification according to the Law of Moses had been completed, Joseph and Mary took him to Jerusalem to present him to the Lord (as is written in the Law of the Lord, "Every first born male is to be consecrated to the Lord"), and to offer a sacrifice in keeping with what is said in the Law of the Lord: "a pair of doves or two young pigeons".

After the birth of a son, a mother had to wait forty days before going to the temple to offer a sacrifice for her purification. This was prescribed in the Law. The actual sacrifice should be:

LEVITICUS
CH. 12, vv. 6-8

a year-old lamb for a burnt offering and a young pigeon or a dove for a sin offering…and then she will be clean

The significance of there being two birds in Joseph's and Mary's sacrifice is explained in Chapter 11, *Birds and Worship*.

Clearly Joseph and Mary were not wealthy. Already as a carpenter Joseph had to leave his workshop and livelihood, journey from Nazareth to Bethlehem, and find lodgings there. In those days that was at least a three-day journey. The journey from Bethlehem to the Temple in Jerusalem was another eight kilometres (five miles) or so, a taxing day out for the young family. All that their resources could manage was to buy the minimum sacrifice of a pair of doves (or two young pigeons which would be small like the doves). So Joseph and Mary did

GOLDEN EAGLE

as the Law demanded and presented their first-born at the Temple to be dedicated to the Lord. First-born animals were also dedicated: they were sacrificed. But a boy's dedication meant that he would serve the Lord throughout his life; as indeed Jesus did. This ritual is a practical thanksgiving of the Faithful as they remember how they were freed from Egypt:

EXODUS
CH. 13, VV. 11-13

After the LORD brings you into the land of the Canaanites and gives it to you, as he promised on oath to you and your forefathers, you are to give over to the LORD the first offspring of every womb. All the firstborn males of your livestock belong to the LORD. Redeem with a lamb every firstborn donkey, but if you do not redeem it, break its neck. Redeem every firstborn among your sons.

From His earliest day Jesus was "touched" by birds. The next great event in His life included a bird too:

ST MATTHEW
CH. 3, VV. 13-17

Then Jesus came from Galilee to the Jordan to be baptised by John. But John tried to deter him, saying, "I need to be baptised by you, and do you come to me?"
Jesus replied, "Let it be so now; it is proper for us to do this to fulfil all righteousness." Then John consented.
As soon as Jesus was baptised, he went up out of the water. At that moment heaven was opened, and he saw the Spirit of God descending like a dove and lighting on him. And a voice from heaven said, "This is my son, whom I love; with him I am well pleased."

This was such an important event in Christ's life and in the recollections of the gospel writers that all four of them record the event, and mention the dove (see also St Mark, ch. 1; St Luke, ch. 3; St John, ch. 1). It is important to notice that they record that the Holy Spirit came upon Jesus "like a dove", but no one saw an actual bird.

This episode was the beginning of Jesus' ministry as the Messiah, the Christ. By His baptism Jesus identified Himself with Man's sin, was an example to His followers and above all showed that He was consecrated by God. There was no spectacular miraculous sight for the crowds who were there to witness. It seems clear from the records that only Jesus and John the Baptist realized the significance of the event. As news of it was passed on, the wonder of the Spirit of God coming on Jesus was described as "like a dove". I think that phrase must have come down to the first followers of Jesus from Jesus Himself. His skill at describing spiritual events by using an everyday image was clear from the beginning of His ministry.

ROCK DOVE

But why was the Holy Spirit like a dove? I feel sure Jesus was familiar with doves as He grew up. He would have learned the scriptures from the rabbi in Nazareth and would have become familiar with how the Spirit of God guided and strengthened His people, how a dove had helped Noah, and that God had a "still, small voice", perhaps like the gentle cooing of a dove. He would have been familiar with the sacrifices of doves at the Temple, and no doubt Mary would have told Him how, as a baby, she and Joseph had sacrificed two when He was dedicated. This familiar bird was an obvious image for Jesus to choose when He felt the need to tell the story of His baptism, and how He had felt filled with the Spirit of God. To His followers later it certainly symbolized much of what Jesus stood for – His gentleness and His sacrificial nature.

Centuries later, the white dove became a symbol of the Christian church, and more particularly of the Holy Spirit of God at work in the world, and was often so depicted in Christian art.

From then on Jesus' ministry took Him to the length and breadth of Palestine, and He taught the Gospel of Love to individuals like the woman at the well in Samaria, to small groups like His twelve disciples and to huge crowds. His teaching sometimes mentioned birds.

During His lifetime Jesus would have seen a great variety of birds in the many habitats He travelled through – in the hills above Galilee (His home, Nazareth, was built on a hill), in the wooded valley of the River Jordan, the palm groves around Jericho, the bare wasteland by the road from Jerusalem to Jericho and around the homes of the many villagers. Pilgrims to the Holy Land today can see many birds which Jesus could have seen – larks, Turtle Doves, eagles and egrets, warblers, Palestine Sunbirds, Swifts and Swallows, Yellow-vented Bulbuls, spectacular Hoopoes, Bee-eaters and Kingfishers. On our pilgrimage a few years ago, from the Golan Heights in the north to the Dead Sea in the south, we saw nearly 80 species, from the mighty Griffon Vulture to the dainty Graceful Warbler. The commonest bird was the House Sparrow that was found wherever we stopped.

PALESTINE
SUNBIRD

This brings us to one of Jesus' earliest recorded teachings that is found in St Matthew's gospel in the Sermon on the Mount. Jesus appeals to His audience not to worry about their lives. They were obviously as worried then about their homes, food, drink and clothes as people often are today:

> **ST MATTHEW**
> CH. 6, VV. 25-27

Therefore I tell you, do not worry about your life, what you will eat or drink; or about your body, what you will wear. Is not life more important than food, and the body more important than clothes? Look at the birds of the air; they do not sow or reap or store away in barns, and yet your heavenly father feeds them. Are you not much more valuable than they? Who of you by worrying can add a single hour to his life?

It is easy to imagine that "the birds of the air" were any or all of the species we have just listed. God looks after them. He will look after us. Jesus clearly tells His audience that. The birds Jesus saw probably did not store food as far as He knew, but careful observation in modern times has revealed that the crow family in many parts of the world does indeed cache food. For example, the Jay of Europe and Asia, which is found in Palestine, even right in the old city of Jerusalem, is a busy hoarder of acorns, burying them in the autumn and searching for them when food is scarce in the winter; and those summer migrants to Palestine, the shrikes, impale insects, even small lizards and mammals, on thorns in bushes. This food is known as the shrike's "larder". If Jesus had known this, I am sure he would have taught His followers that, even as God has shown birds how to take care of food, so they (and we today) should do the same.

Sometime later Jesus sent out the twelve disciples with careful instructions, and further exhortation to trust God for all the strength they needed. He emphasized this with a reference to birds again:

> **ST MATTHEW**
> CH. 10, V. 29

Are not five sparrows sold for two pennies? Yet not one of them will fall to the ground apart from the will of your Father.

HOUSE SPARROW

St Luke records the event slightly differently:

> **ST LUKE**
> CH. 12, V. 6

Are not five sparrows sold for two pennies? Yet not one of them is forgotten by God. Indeed, the very hairs of your head are all numbered. Don't be afraid; you are worth more than many sparrows.

EURASIAN
JAY

It seems that the usual market price was two birds a penny, but they were so cheap that a bargain price could be had at five for twopence. The original word Luke used for the coin was "assarion" for the Roman coin, the assarius. This was the next to smallest coin, which emphasizes how cheap the birds were in the market. The message is the same, whichever Gospel version we read – not even the least of God's creatures is outside God's care. This would have been a very striking message for the disciples to hear who had lowly jobs and lived poor lives when compared with the wealthy Romans whom they no doubt saw daily and the opulent life of their priests. These small birds taught the disciples an early lesson in the richness of God's love.

St Luke's and St Matthew's original Greek word, which has been translated as "sparrows" ever since the 17th century's Authorised Version, was the plural "strouthia", (singular "strouthion"). The Hebrew equivalent then for small bird was "tsippor". The contemporary Hebrew name for the House Sparrow is "dror habayit". All the modern Bibles translate it as Sparrow, as is recorded in Woodhouse's *English/Greek Dictionary,* first published in 1910. House Sparrows certainly are common in the Holy Land, and make an ideal image in Jesus' message.

Jesus said several things to His twelve disciples to help them with the evangelical work they had to do. When He first sent them out to "drive out evil spirits and to heal every disease and sickness" (St Matthew, ch. 10, v. 1) he said to them, "I am sending you out like sheep among wolves. Therefore be as shrewd as snakes and as innocent as doves" (St Matthew, ch. 10, v. 16). They had to combat the evil in the world and argue against unbelievers, not with bullying or guile or lies but with the wisdom that snakes proverbially had, and with the gentleness of doves. Later, in one of the last bits of advice He gave His disciples, He warned them of the troubles there would be in the world at His Second Coming. They must beware of false claims that He has returned, but must look for the sure sign:

ST MATTHEW
CH. 24, VV. 27-28

For as lightning that comes from the east is visible even in the west, so will be the coming of the Son of Man. Wherever there is a carcass, there the vultures will gather".

Jesus clearly well knew the habits of vultures. They would have been a common sight in His time during all His travels. In this instance they were a perfect illustration for what the end of the world would be like on Judgment Day, as was generally believed at that time.

Although Jesus named only a few particular species, His observations authoritatively speak of God's love for everyone. He emphasizes this with the telling question when He is teaching the disciples about prayer:

 ST LUKE
CH. 11, vv. 11-12

Which of you fathers, if your son asks for a fish, will give him a snake instead? Or if he asks for an egg, will give him a scorpion? If you then, though you are evil, know how to give good gifts to your children, how much more will your Father in heaven give the Holy Spirit to those who ask him!

Wild birds' eggs as well as hens' eggs would have been familiar food for the disciples who should have quickly grasped the point of Jesus' message. One of the most familiar sounds in Palestine must have been the early morning crowing of a cockerel. In Chapter 3 we have read that early in man's stewardship of Creation, Jungle Fowl were tamed and spread to the Middle East and Europe, and these birds were spoken of by Jesus in one of His most emotional speeches:

ST LUKE
CH. 13, v. 34

O Jerusalem, Jerusalem, you who kill the prophets and stone those who are sent to you, how often I have longed to gather your children together, as a hen gathers her chicks under her wings, but you were not willing!

This picture is so sharply observed that thoughtful hearers would have sensed Jesus' distress. God had, over the years, looked after the Jews despite their sinful lapses. Now Jesus' words and actions, bringing hope, healing and love, had already created disunity among His disciples, the Samaritans had scorned Him, King Herod wanted to kill Him, He had angered Pharisees; and the nation itself, as Jesus had exclaimed here, had spurned the words of God's messengers, Himself included. Even His Gospel of Love could not gather everyone together as He wished. The sight of a hen and her chicks and the sound of the cockerel gave Jesus simple but striking pictures to illustrate what He had to say. The cock's crowing also featured in one of the most dramatic events at the end of His earthly life, as we will read later in this chapter.

As Jesus walked with His disciples through the Palestinian countryside He was very aware of the work farmers were doing in the fields, sowing, harvesting and caring for their animals, such as sheep and goats. His observant attention to what was going on gave Him ideas that enabled Him to explain certain aspects of His Good News. For example, He told parables (about thirty are recorded in the Gospels), "earthly stories with a heavenly meaning", stories which used illustrations from nature and human life to explain what God's message was. We call one of the best-known "The Parable of the Sower". It clearly made a big impression on the early disciples because it is recorded in all three of the Synoptic Gospels – Matthew, Mark and Luke. In those days a farmer sowed barley or wheat by throwing handfuls of seed from a basket, with a sweeping movement of his arm – the technical word for that is "broadcasting" – on to the ploughed soil:

ST MATTHEW
CH. 12, vv. 3-8

As a farmer went out to sow his seed, some fell along the path, and the birds came and ate it up. Some fell on rocky places... Other seed fell among the thorns... Still others fell on good soil, where it produced a good crop.

The disciples did not understand what Jesus meant so He had to explain at length how the people who hear God's message listen to it and understand it in different ways, but only those who are really paying attention will properly reap the benefit of what they have heard. Many birds in Jesus' experience would have followed the farmer and pecked at the seed – House Sparrows, finches, doves, crows and larks. He had to explain that the part about the birds represented anyone who, when he "hears the message about the kingdom and does not understand it, the evil one comes and snatches away what was sown in his heart. This is the seed sown along the path" (St Matthew, ch. 12, v. 19).

During the Feast of the Passover, at the end of Jesus' earthly ministry, He shared His last meal with His disciples. Afterwards:

ST MATTHEW
CH. 26 vv. 30-35

...they went out to the Mount of Olives.

[SEE ALSO ST MARK, CH. 14, ST LUKE, CH, 22, ST JOHN, CH. 18]

Swallow

They all rested that night in the Garden of Gethsemane. The disciples slept while Jesus prayed. He found them asleep and challenged Peter in particular:

 ST MATTHEW
CH. 26, VV. 40-41

"Could you men not keep watch with me for one hour?" he asked Peter. "Watch and pray so that you will not fall into temptation. The spirit is willing, but the body is weak."

And they *were* weak. They fled when Jesus was arrested, but Peter at least followed Him and was found sitting in the courtyard outside the High Priest's house where Jesus was being questioned. When asked, he denied three times that he knew Jesus. At that moment the cock crowed, and Peter, remembering how Jesus had said, "Before the cock crows you will disown me three times" (St Matthew, ch. 26, v. 75), wept bitterly. Once again Jesus had mentioned something commonplace, and from it a great truth had sprung. Jesus and Peter may even have had in mind the ancient writer's message that one of the four things that was impressive to watch as they walk was "the strutting cocks" (Proverbs, ch. 30, v. 31). The truth of his fear and his trying to strut through life without Jesus stung Peter, and thereafter his witness for Christ and His message really did live up to his being the rock on which Christ's church would be built. Peter's experience was described in the 12th century manuscript, *The Roxburgh Bestiary*:

"At [the cock's] crowing the devoted mind rises to prayer and the priest begins again to read his office. By testifying devotedly after cock-crow Peter washed away the sin of the Church, which he had incurred by denying Christ before it crowed. It is by this song that hope returns to the sick, trouble is turned to advantage, the pain of wounds is relieved, the burning of fever is lessened, faith is restored to the fallen, Christ turns his face to the wavering or reforms the erring, wandering of mind departs and negation is driven out. Confession follows. Scripture teaches that this did not happen by chance, but by the will of our lord."

Domestic Cock

Today, Christ's followers must heed the signs that God gives them as carefully as did the medieval writer, so that they do not repeatedly deny the truth.

SACRED IBIS

After Christ's death and resurrection His followers eventually wrote down His life's story in the Gospels and encouraged each other by sharing letters and other writings. They, too, occasionally mentioned birds. Paul reminded his readers of the times when people forsook God and created idols of gods of their own devising:

 ROMANS
CH. 1, V. 23

Although [men] claimed to be wise, they became fools and exchanged the glory of the immortal God for images made to look like mortal man and birds and animals and reptiles. ⟳

Paul's audience would have been very familiar in their time with Greek and Roman temples and idols to many gods. Many of his listeners may well have known how in ancient Egypt the falcon and the ibis were sacred. For several centuries the Jews had been influenced by Greek culture and language. Educated people for whom Paul was writing would very likely have heard the story of how the god Zeus took the shape of a swan in order to woo Leda. Perhaps St Paul had these in mind as he wrote to those Christians in Rome. Even today we must beware of creating false gods and appearing foolish. In another letter, Paul discusses the nature of the resurrection and so he writes about the natural body and the spiritual body. The former he describes like this:

 1 CORINTHIANS
CH. 15, V. 39

All flesh is not the same: Men have one kind of flesh, animals have another, birds another and fish another. ⟳

The argument comes to a climax in the famous lines:

1 CORINTHIANS
CH. 15, VV. 51-54

Listen. I tell you a mystery: We will not all sleep, but we will all be changed. For the perishable must clothe itself with the imperishable, and the mortal with immortality. When the perishable has been clothed with the imperishable, and the mortal with immortality, then the saying that is written will come true: "Death has been swallowed up in victory". ⟳

Although Paul does not name a particular species, he was well aware of God's Creation: that birds in general could teach us a truth about our relationship with God, about our lives here on earth and about the life to come.

The writer of Revelation speaks of the mighty eagle in Chapter 8, and, at the beginning of Chapter 18, of "every unclean and detestable bird", which finds a home in "Babylon the Great" (which may mean Jerusalem, or the world generally). But the richest reference to birds outside the Gospels is in the story of an experience that St Peter had. He was staying at the house of Simon the tanner in Joppa, a town on the Mediterranean coast, north-west of Jerusalem:

ACTS OF THE APOSTLES
CH. 10, vv. 9-16

About noon the following day as they [the two servants of Cornelius the centurion] were on their journey and approaching the city, Peter went up on the roof to pray [it was quite usual for houses to have flat roofs, and an outside staircase. It was a convenient place to relax and be private]. He became hungry and wanted something to eat, and while the meal was being prepared he fell into a trance. He saw heaven opened and something like a large sheet being let down to earth by its four corners. It contained all kinds of four-legged animals, as well as reptiles of the earth and birds of the air. Then a voice told him, "Get up, Peter; kill and eat."

"Surely not, Lord!" Peter replied. "I have never eaten anything impure and unclean."

The voice spoke to him a second time, "Do not call anything impure that God has made clean."

This happened three times, and immediately the sheet was taken back to heaven.

Cornelius, the centurion of Caesarea, to the north of Joppa, also had had a vision, which is why he had sent the two servants to find Peter. They took him back to Cornelius who wanted Peter to tell him "everything the Lord has commanded you to tell us".

Peter by this time had worked out what his vision meant and said to Cornelius:

🖋 ACTS OF THE
APOSTLES
CH. 10, VV. 28-29

You are well aware that it is against our law for a Jew to associate with a Gentile or visit him. But God has shown me that I should not call any man impure or unclean. So when I was sent for, I came without raising any objection. 🖋

IMMATURE GOLDEN EAGLE

GREY HERON: UNCLEAN

Peter preached to Cornelius' entire household. The Holy Spirit came on all who heard his message and they were all baptised in the name of Jesus. Peter's story, recorded by Luke, speaks of birds in the same spirit that Jesus mentioned them – to illustrate a great truth of the Gospel of Love, that God loves everyone, a fact picked up by words of St Paul:

> ROMANS *For there is no difference between Jew and Gentle*
> CH. 10, v. 12 *– the same Lord is Lord of all.*

He emphasized this in his first letter to the Corinthians where he stated that with people who believe in Christ, there is no racial or cultural or social distinction – we are all one. Small, seemingly insignificant birds like sparrows alighting in the Palestinian fields, or feeding on the fallen seed by people's homes, or being sold for food in the markets, may have been a common sight, but Jesus and his apostles saw in them a rich example of God's love for all Creation, and that included all men, women and children, Jews and Gentiles.

CRESTED LARKS:
CLEAN

CHAPTER VIII

SINGING AND NESTING BIRDS

Many people are excited by the sight of a brilliantly plumaged bird – the flash of blue when a Kingfisher flies by, the astounding fan of a Peacock's tail, the wonderful flicker of colours as a Goldfinch lands on the bird table. In my experience, however, fewer folk get excited by the *sound* of a bird. The non-stop mournful cooing of a dove is, I know, irritating to some people, the Raven's croak is ugly and the cacophony of sound at a seabird colony is not music! Nevertheless birdsong *has* attracted the attention of sensitive men and women. One of the oldest songs in English, from c.1250, says:

> *Summer is icumen in,*
> *Lhudhe sing cuccu !*

The repeated notes of the European Cuckoo were a clear sign that winter was over, so let us all join in! Fifteen hundred years before that anonymous songwriter was inspired by a bird, Theocritus, the Greek pastoral poet, wrote "Larks and finches sang, the dove made moan, and bees flitted humming above the springs. All things were fragrant of rich harvest and fruit time."

But even that is not old compared with what we can find in the Old Testament of the Bible. Even as the writer in the Middle Ages in England had been inspired by the end of winter's cold and the coming of summer's warmth, so was the Psalmist who observed "The birds of the air... they sing among the branches" (Psalm 104, v. 12).

He was writing before the exile to Babylon, so his hymn to the Creator may have been composed as many as 3,000 years ago. Sadly there is only one other reference to song in the Bible that we read in Chapter 1 (page 16) in a slightly different translation:

> *For now the winter is past,*
> *the rains are over and gone;*
> *the flowers appear in the countryside;*
> *the time is coming when the birds will sing,*
> *and the turtle dove's cooing will be*
> *heard in our land.* ❧

⤳ SONG OF SONGS

CH. 2, vv. 11-12

NEW ENGLISH BIBLE

Male (left) and Female lesser Kestrels

PALESTINIAN SONGBIRDS

| BIRDS OF THE BIBLE

With these words the Beloved appeals to her Lover. He replies with another, gentle image of a dove:

 SONG OF
SONGS
CH. 2, V. 14

My dove in the clefts of the rock,
in the hiding places on the mountainside,
show me your face,
let me hear your voice;
for your voice is sweet,
and your face is lovely.

Thus the lovers really were well aware of, firstly, what was surely the soothing, purring song of a Turtle Dove, and secondly of the "sweet" cooing of the Rock Dove. Together these blissful images convince the Beloved that " My lover is mine and I am his" (Song of Songs, ch. 2, v. 16):

I do not find it surprising that there are so few references to birdsong, as Alice Parmelee remarked in her book. Birdsong is not heard by many people, even though it is there, because they do not "tune in" to it. I find it more surprising when I have been leading a birdwatching walk if someone asks, "What was that song?"

In spring there is plenty of birdsong in Palestine, in the fields, in the hills, by the River Jordan, and even in the villages and towns. In just the first two days of a stay in Jerusalem in mid-April I heard Palm Doves cooing, Swifts screaming in their courtship flights, several Yellow-vented Bulbuls singing – their powerful, rich, flutey notes ringing across the roofs of Jerusalem – a Great Tit singing *teacher-teacher* in the Garden of Gethsemane, in the leafy sanctuary of the Garden Tomb, a Blackbird, a Greenfinch and a Palestine Sunbird singing – the last in a flowering Judas Tree; and in the gardens and scrub the common Sardinian Warblers with their bold, chattering song. So, I think there would have been plenty of birdsong to listen to in the Psalmist's and Christ's time – if they had been as aware of that as they were of their own music which the Psalmist writes about in Psalms 98 and 150.

Although birds' songs did not attract the attention of the Bible's authors, some birds' calls did. Whereas in Song of Songs the dove's cooing was a lovely sound, the prophets had different ideas about what birds' calls meant for them. Only the lovers heard songs; it seems that most Israelites had been so oppressed by warring neighbours, and had suffered for so long in Exile in the seventh century BC, that certain birdcalls were not described as being pleasant, they were sad or ominous.

The prophet Micah, who wrote some years before 700 BC, lived in the kingdom of Judah in the southern part of the Holy Land. He observed the people's sinfulness and lack of service to God. He prophesied that Samaria and Jerusalem would fall and:

➣ MICAH
CH. 1, vv. 8-9

Because of this I will weep and wail;
I will go about barefoot and naked.
I will howl like a jackal
and moan like an owl.
For her wound is incurable... ➣

Between 734 and 701 BC the Assyrians did invade, and conquer as far south as Jerusalem which was spared from destruction. Zephaniah, who prophesied about a hundred years later, was also from Judah and was a descendant of King Hezekiah who was the last king whom Micah knew. Once again he writes that God is about to punish apostate Judah, but the Lord eventually will destroy those who threaten Israel and Judah:

➣ ZEPHANIAH
CH. 2, v. 14

The desert owl and the screech owl
will roost in her columns.
Their calls will echo through the windows,
rubble will be in the doorways... ➣

Owl

Many modern translations agree that owls will be hooting through the windows but there is little agreement on how to translate the proper names of the birds; and the "rubble" of the New International Version is a bird in other translations! We read of the "horned owl and ruffed bustard" (New English Bible), "tawny owl" will hoot in the window (New English Bible) and a "bustard" (New English Bible) or a "raven" (New Revised Standard Version) will "croak on the threshold". The New English Bible's choice of "bustard" here is curious. Bustards are birds of open grassland; two species are rare in Israel today, through loss of habitat and over-hunting. Even at the best of times a bustard seems an unlikely bird to be seen in the ruined doorway of an Assyrian house. But the mournful sound of an owl, especially the deep *ooo-hooo, ooo-hooo* of the Eagle Owl, would undoubtedly have been a sinister sound that emphasized the desolation of a ruined city. These owls are still widespread in Israel. Their call is often made just as they leave a roost at dusk to go hunting. The call is so loud that on a still night it carries two to three kilometres (a mile or so). That would certainly have greatly affected impressionable people.

Curiously the dove's cooing was not only a sign of love as we have seen, but was also thought of as mournful enough to be used as a simile to describe someone's sorrow. In the sixth century BC Ezekiel had a vision that "The end has come upon the four corners of the land.... All who survive and escape will be in the mountains, moaning like doves of the valleys" (Ezekiel, ch. 7,

HOUBARA BUSTARD

vv. 2 & 16). About 700 BC, King Hezekiah was ill; he felt near to death; it seemed as if his bones were broken and he bemoaned his state of health at length: "I moaned like a mourning dove" (Isaiah, ch. 38, v. 14). Later, the prophet describes the people's miserable state in grim terms:

SARDINIAN WARBLER

ISAIAH
CH. 59, VV. 10 & 11

At midday we stumble as if it were twilight;
among the strong we are like the dead.
We all growl like bears;
We moan mournfully like doves.
We look for justice but find none...

Even today some people consider the repetitive cooing of a dove, such as the Collared Dove, as less than pleasant (or much worse!). It is easy to think of the sound as funereal. Indeed, the most widespread and abundant dove in the United States is called the Mourning Dove because of its mournful call. It is about the size of a Collared or Turtle Dove. The Collared's call (or song) is particularly repetitive and mournful, but that species may not have been so widespread in ancient times in Palestine as it is now. So Ezekiel and Isaiah were more likely to be hearing Rock Doves. But owls and doves are not the only birds with calls that distress people. In Australia the Pallid Cuckoo has a mating call, repeated day and night, which one writer says sends some people near to screaming point!

Our last mention of a calling or singing bird is an unusual one. Among God's great list of questions to Job is a series about the huge marine animal that he calls "Leviathan", and one of the questions asks:

> JOB
CH. 41, V. 5   *Can you make a pet of him like a bird?*

This is the only reference in the scriptures to cage birds, but it is a fascinating insight into what was probably daily life in Palestine. Although the Bible record does not say much about the joy people can feel from hearing birdsong, this one question implies that songbirds in cages were a familiar sight in ancient times. Other ancient historical records mention them. King Hezekiah of Judah in the seventh century BC was besieged in Jerusalem "like a caged bird". Other people who lived by the Mediterranean also kept cage birds as is shown on classical Greek vases that are 2,500 years old. Anyone who has recently been on holiday there will have seen little cages hanging on the walls of the houses, with maybe a Canary as we would have at home, but often a Goldfinch or a Bullfinch. The Yellow-vented Bulbuls of Palestine are not beautifully coloured but they are handsomely marked, their white eye-rings bright against the black head, and the bright yellow under the tail in great contrast to the grey-brown plumage. They are talkative birds! Their natural flute-like song is enhanced by a wide range of calls that mimic other species. They are a very noticeable feature of Palestinian birdsong, as we have already read in Chapter 1, and could well be the species God had in mind.

Although birdsong is not well recorded in the Bible, birds' nests are. A spring trip to Palestine today can be a "bird-nesting experience" for an observant pilgrim. Over a few days in spring I have seen a Common Kestrel feeding young under the roof tiles of the Church of the Holy Sepulchre, a pair of Lesser Kestrels mating near a nest-hole on the Wailing Wall and a Palm Dove building a nest on a ledge above the entrance to the Garden Tomb; a Blackstart was feeding young in a drainpipe nest-hole at Qumran and Red-rumped Swallows were nesting in ruins at the Pool of Banias (the site of Caesarea Philippi).

Swallow

People living in the Holy Land must have been very aware of the birds nesting nearby. What is particularly impressive about what the Bible says about this is that the people of the Promised Land were from the beginning very conscious about conservation as is recorded in the fifth and last book of the Pentateuch:

DEUTERONOMY
CH. 20, V. 19

When you lay siege to a city for a long time, fighting against it to capture it, do not destroy its trees by putting an axe to them, because you can eat their fruit. Do not cut them down. Are the trees of the field people, that you should besiege them? ...

Trees provide wood for building, fruit to eat and nest-sites for birds. Chapter 20 does not specifically save the trees for birds, but a later Law does have "conservation" (as we would say today) in mind:

DEUTERONOMY
CH. 22, VV. 6-7

If you come across a bird's nest beside the road, either in a tree or on the ground, and the mother is sitting on the young or on the eggs, do not take the mother with the young. You may take the young, but be sure to let the mother go, so that it may go well with you and you may have a long life.

This is a very sensible law which in modern times has not been followed in many parts of the world where animals and birds have been hunted to extinction, forests have been destroyed, and no attention has been given to there being a "harvest" for future generations to enjoy – a quick profit now has been the only rule.

The Psalmist records the importance of the trees of Palestine and accurately names the stork as a tree nester; it would be the White Stork he had in mind:

PSALM
104, VV. 16-17

The trees of the Lord are well watered, the cedars of Lebanon that he planted. There the birds make their nests; the stork has its home in the pine trees.

The Prophet Jeremiah complained bitterly about the sinfulness of men that resulted in a devastated landscape in which wildlife suffered:

⮐ JEREMIAH
CH. 12, VV. 1-4

You are always righteous, O Lord
when I bring a case before you.
Yet I would speak to you about your justice:
Why does the way of the wicked prosper?
Why do all the faithless live at ease?
You have planted them, and they have taken root;
they grow and bear fruit.
You are always on their lips
but far from their hearts.
Yet you know me, O Lord;
you see me and test my thoughts about you.
Drag them off like sheep to be butchered!
Set them apart for the day of slaughter!
How long will the land lie parched
and the grass in every field be withered?
Because those who live in it are wicked,
the animals and birds have perished. ⮐

Many centuries later, Jeremiah's words still ring true; the dreadful wars in several parts of Asia, the Middle East and Africa are witness to them. The most interesting references to the importance of trees are with regard to the Cedar of Lebanon that was a rich source of building material. Way back in about 960 BC, Solomon began the building of his Temple, and asked Hiram, the friendly King of Tyre, to provide wood to help build it:

⮐ 1 KINGS
CH. 5, VV. 7-8

When Hiram heard Solomon's message, he was
greatly pleased and said, " Praise be to the lord
today, for he has given David a wise son to rule
over his great nation." So Hiram sent word to
Solomon: I have received the message you sent me
and will do all you want in providing the cedar
and pine logs he wanted. ⮐

These trees were huge, the largest in the Holy Land. They grow slowly, live to a great age and may reach a height of 30 m (100 ft). They clearly were a very valuable resource to be conserved with good stewardship, for several reasons, not just for sites for birds' nests. King Nebuchadnezzar of Babylon, who ruled from 605–562 BC, had a vision about a huge tree early on in his reign, which he described to Daniel:

DANIEL
CH. 4, VV. 9-12 & 19-22

Here is my dream; interpret it for me. These are the visions I saw while lying in my bed: I looked, and there before me stood a tree in the middle of the land. Its height was enormous. The tree grew large and strong and its top touched the sky; it was visible to the ends of the earth. Its leaves were beautiful, its fruit abundant, and on it was food for all. Under it the birds of the field found shelter, and the birds of the air lived in its branches; from it every creature was fed...[Daniel answered:] My Lord, if only the dream applied to your enemies and its meaning to your adversaries! The tree you saw, which grew large and strong, with its top touching the sky, visible to the whole earth, with beautiful leaves and abundant fruit, providing food for all, giving shelter to the beasts of the field, and having nesting places in its branches for the birds of the air - you, O king are that tree! You have become great and strong; your greatness has grown until it reaches the sky, and your dominion extends to distant parts of the earth.

This was a vision that Daniel interpreted for him as portraying the all-embracing nature of his great kingdom, but the tree would be reduced to a stump and the king too would suffer for his sins (as indeed he did). His tree was probably a Cedar. By this time the huge forests – and birds' nest-sites – were being decimated by war and for building materials, despite the Law (as we have read in Deuteronomy). The leading prophets proclaimed that the wickedness of men was the cause of the desolate landscape. Where the Cedars had been felled the land was bare; where that bare land had been tilled and terraced even that was laid bare again by war; Jeremiah complained bitterly:

 JEREMIAH
CH. 12, V. 4

How long will the land lie parched
and the grass in every field be withered?
Because those who lived in it are wicked,
the animals and birds have perished.

I feel sure Jeremiah was thinking not only of farm animals and birds, but also about the wild creatures that had suffered, just as is happening today in many countries, including our own. God's answer to Jeremiah was a grim description of how He felt because His people had been so wicked:

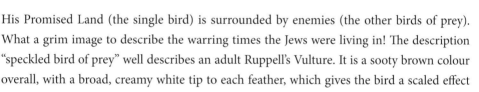 JEREMIAH
CH. 12, V. 9

Has not my inheritance become to me
like a speckled bird of prey
that other birds of prey surround and attack?

His Promised Land (the single bird) is surrounded by enemies (the other birds of prey). What a grim image to describe the warring times the Jews were living in! The description "speckled bird of prey" well describes an adult Ruppell's Vulture. It is a sooty brown colour overall, with a broad, creamy white tip to each feather, which gives the bird a scaled effect from above and a speckled appearance from below. God's Chosen People had so openly and comprehensively rejected God's laws that here they are described as a bird which Jeremiah's listeners would have immediately recognized as "unclean". What a damning description to hear of yourself! Today, this species is widespread in Africa from Egypt, southwards down through the Rift Valley, but although there are reports from Sinai, there are none nearer the Promised Land than that.

In a hymn in praise of and longing for the Temple by a Psalmist who was denied access to it during the ravaging of Judah by Sennacherib in 701 BC (described in 2 Kings, ch. 18), we read this:

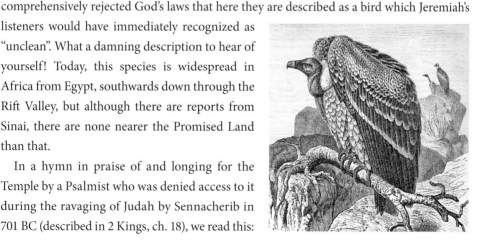

RUPPELL'S VULTURE

How lovely is your dwelling place,
O Lord Almighty!
My soul yearns, even faints,
for the courts of the lord;

PSALM
84, vv. 1-4

my heart and flesh cry out for the living God.
Even the sparrow has found a home,
and the swallow a nest for herself.
where she may have her young -
a place near your altar,
O Lord almighty, my King and my God.

LESSER KESTREL

Even though the writer, probably a Levite who would have normally officiated in the Temple, is distressed because he cannot go into the Temple, he is near enough and observant enough to see the birds which do gain access, or he is remembering what he has seen in the past when he was able to go into the Temple – and the birds' finding a "home" emphasizes his distress. Both the House Sparrow and the Swallow do nest in buildings; House Sparrows are often found in a loose colony, in holes in a wall or under roof tiles. The wild site for a Swallow would have been a cave entrance, where it would stick its mud nest to a ledge, but since time immemorial Swallows have nested in man-made structures such as barns, bridges, church porches and sheds – or temples. The Psalmist may have seen either a Barn Swallow (the one we usually call simply "Swallow") or a Red-rumped Swallow, or both because they commonly nest in buildings.

Edomites who lived south of the Dead Sea opposed Israel at every opportunity but their destruction, as Isaiah prophesied, would come about:

BARN
SWALLOW

⤳ ISAIAH

CH. 34, VV. 9-15

Edom's streams will be turned into pitch,
her dust into burning sulphur;
her land will become blazing pitch!
It will not be quenched night and day;
its smoke will rise for ever.
From generation to generation it will lie desolate;
no-one will ever pass through it again.
The desert owl and screech owl will possess it;
the great owl and the raven will nest there.......
The owl will nest there and lay eggs,
she will hatch them, and care for her young
under the shadow of her wings;
there also the falcons will gather each its mate. ⤳

The land's desolation is emphasized by the prophet's listing of such grim, "unclean" birds of doom as the Owls and the Raven, although it must be admitted that the original Hebrew is unclear for the first three owls' names and so this translation is conjecture; other translations name Cormorant, Bittern, Ostrich, Buzzard and Hawk! It does, however, seem certain that Isaiah was intent on describing Edom's downfall as grimly as possible – with a list of the "unclean birds" which will inhabit the land. I feel much more sure in suggesting that the "falcons" (if that is the right translation) are Lesser Kestrels. They are summer migrants to the

Middle East and Asia eastwards to China. They nest in colonies, commonly of fifteen to twenty pairs, but maybe only two or three, or even up to a hundred or more. The breeding site now is usually a high building, old walls or fortifications, as no doubt it was centuries ago – just the sort of bird that would nest in the ruins of Babylon or Ninevah that Isaiah prophesied would be there. Today the species is much less common than it used to be. The birds are mainly insect feeders and many populations have been hard hit by the extensive use of modern pesticides on farmland; the falcons have not been able to find enough to eat. In Israel, before the 1950s, there used to be several colonies of hundreds of pairs, such as those at Safed and in Rosh Hankra near Galilee, but now there is a total national population of only a few hundred. However, with a more satisfactory stewardship of the land their numbers are increasing.

Jeremiah, too, prophesied Edom's defeat. His message from the Lord was that: "Though you build your nest as high as the eagle's, from there I will bring you down" (Jeremiah, ch. 49, v. 16). An eagle's eyrie is an impressive stick construction that usually is on an inaccessible ledge high on a cliff. Though so well protected it is clearly visible, as undoubtedly Jeremiah had noticed, because it is so huge a nest – it may be two metres (six and a half feet) deep and have a diameter of one and a half metres (five feet). Tree nests are even bigger.

The Old Testament records two proverbs that describe bird behaviour to help explain a man's actions:

PROVERBS *Like a bird that strays from its nest.*
CH. 27, V. 8 *Is a man who strays from his home.*

The man, like the bird, has lost his security; the nest and the home could be robbed. Jeremiah also gave a warning about the likely punishment in chapter 17, verse 11 (see page 52).

Doves feature strongly in the books of the Old and New Testaments. God, speaking through the words of the Prophet Jeremiah, cries against Israel's invaders:

Abandon your towns and dwell among the rocks,
JEREMIAH *you who live in Moab.*
CH. 48, V. 28 *Be like a dove that makes its nest*
at the mouth of a cave.

This is a perfect description of a wild Rock Dove's nest site. Unlike the Turtle Doves and the Palm (or Laughing) Doves of the farmed lands, this member of the family, throughout its range, nests in clefts in rocks, cliffs and cave entrances. It is common wherever rocks, some vegetation, and permanent water occur, even in deserts where the Desert Melon grows which can provide food and water. But what a dreadful place for Moabites to live!

CHUKAR

Osprey on nest

Perhaps the most telling mention of bird's nests, especially for a Christian, is found in a statement made by Jesus:

 ST MATTHEW
CH. 8, vv. 18-22

When Jesus saw the crowd around him, he gave orders to cross to the other side of the lake. Then a teacher of the law came to him and said, "Teacher, I will follow you wherever you go." Jesus replied,. "Foxes have holes and birds of the air have nests, but the Son of Man has nowhere to lay his head."

The man who said he wanted to follow Jesus had no idea of the cost involved when he spoke; perhaps he was just carried away by Jesus' popularity and wanted to be part of it. He was a teacher of the Law, a scribe who probably voiced what many in the crowd were thinking. They must have had a shock when they heard Jesus' reply. Their comfortable security would be gone; they would be in an alien world; they needed to make a huge change in their lives. Jesus firmly and clearly pointed out that following him would cost them dearly in terms of time, comfort and social status – wild animals and birds would be living more comfortably. That is still true today for Jesus' followers, especially in countries where they are persecuted, as they were in the first century AD.

Jesus found other rich sources of imagery from birds besides what we have already found in Chapter 7. Preachers of many Christian denominations nowadays still follow the examples of Jesus and the prophets and teach valuable lessons which are illustrated by the lives of birds.

CRESTED LARK

CHAPTER IX

THE MIGRATION OF BIRDS

O ne of the most noticeable features of bird behaviour all around the world is that they can be seen at certain times of the year, and then they disappear. The most striking examples through the ages have been the spring and summer appearances in the Northern Hemisphere of Swallows, which have wintered in Africa, and later, wildfowl from the far north arriving to spend the winter in temperate countries further south. Earlier generations than ours treasured the arrival of these birds – the Swallows brought the warmth of summer after winter's hard times, and the wildfowl in winter were a source of food in times of need. But where the birds were for the rest of the year was a mystery. As late as the 17th and 18th centuries strange theories were published about where Swallows go. For example, in AD 1750, George Edwards wrote in *A Natural History of Birds* about the summer arrival of cliff-nesting auks in northern islands of Europe, and their later disappearance:

> *I think the most rational Conjecture, of the Manner of their hiding themselves, and being preserved during the long and cold Winters of those climates, is, that there are Sub-marine caverns in the rocky Shores of those Islands, the Mouths of which Caverns, though they be under Water, may lead to hollows, so rising within Side as to afford a convenient dry Harbour, fit to preserve these Birds in a kind of torpid State during the Winter... I cannot solve the disappearance of these Birds any other Way.*

Other writers still thought that Swallows spent the winter so, and the winter-arriving Barnacle Geese were believed to hatch from the black and white sea-barnacles. Israel now is well known as being part of the path of a major migration route from Europe to Africa. Birds migrate from Europe and north-west Asia through a narrow corridor which gives them only a short sea crossing at the eastern end of the Mediterranean, and then they move south through the great Rift Valley into East Africa. The details and truth of the miracle of this migration route have come to light only since the travels of 19th and 20th century explorers and scientists.

Canon Tristram, who published the first detailed accounts of Israel's birds in *The Natural History of the Bible* (1867) and *The Fauna and Flora of Palestine* (1884), wrote of what he saw

HONEY BUZZARD

and heard one spring day in the upper Jordan Valley:

The thickets abounded in francolin, while the
valley itself seems to be the highway of all the
migratory birds returning from their African
winter quarters to western Asia and Russia. Bands
of storks, masses of starlings, clouds of swallows,
long lines of swifts and bee-eaters may be seen hour
after hour ceaselessly passing northwards overhead,
while the surface of the plain is alive with countless
myriads of familiar songsters in loose, scattered
order, hopping, feeding, taking short flights, but
all pursuing their northward course.

Today, birdwatchers flock to Eilat, a modern resort at the southern tip of the Negev Desert in Israel, on the shores of the Red Sea. Solomon had a fleet of ships here; the Queen of Sheba probably landed here when she came to visit Solomon (*1 Kings*, ch. 9 & 10). But they were interested in power and wealth and probably had not noticed that: "Eilat is one of the best places on earth for birdwatching, a twitcher's delight. Migration times are twice a year: from September through November the birds head south to Africa, and from March through May they head back north to Europe" (*Discover Israel*, by Carlton Reid, published by Berlitz).

Solomon and Sheba may have noticed the migratory birds; we shall never know. But three Old Testament writers do give us a view from those far-off days. The prophet Hosea, who was from the northern kingdom of Israel in the middle of the eighth century BC, lived through very troubled times especially when the Assyrians to the north were aggressively attacking the region. Finally, in 722–721 BC, the northern kingdom came to an end and the people were exiled. Hosea speaks for God, describing the nation's sin and lack of repentance, but later he speaks about God's love for his people and prophesies that they will return from exile:

HOSEA
CH. 11, V. 11

they will come trembling
like birds from Egypt,
like doves from Assyria.
I will settle them in their homes,
declares the Lord.

Hosea sees the Israelites' return as being as speedy and as noticeable as the arrival of migrating birds. Many years before that the writer of the book of Job had composed an even more obvious reference to migration in one of the questions that God asks Job:

JOB
CH. 39, V. 26

Does the hawk take flight by your wisdom
and spread his wings towards the south?

LEVANT SPARROWHAWK

One of the most spectacular aspects of migration through the Holy Land is the vast number of birds of prey that pass through each spring and autumn. Eagles, falcons and hawks are all involved. Two species of hawks in particular pass through – the Common Buzzard and Levant Sparrowhawk. The former in modern times is the commonest migrating raptor in spring; more than 100,000 were counted passing over Eilat on one day in March 1980; it is not so common in autumn. But the Levant Sparrowhawks migrate in autumn, going south as God said, in flocks of hundreds or even thousands. The climax is in the third week of September when between 1,000 and 3,000 have been counted in one day at Kafar Kasem on the western slopes of the central mountain range. This route was not discovered by modern ornithologists until 1977, but it seems clear that the writer of Job knew all about it. A Levant Sparrowhawk seems to be the most likely species for the hawk named in verse 26. An individual ringed by scientists in Eilat was found two years later in Romania. Although we have seen that the naming of birds by the ancient writers has created problems for modern translators, the identification of this bird as a "hawk" is secure. The Bible has the word "nets"; in modern Hebrew the hawks are all "nets" (or "nez" as a modern bird list spells it), plus a qualifying adjective.

The most detailed mention of migratory birds is to be found early on in Jeremiah's prophecy. He began his ministry in 626 BC, and preached and prophesied for about another forty years. As with the other prophets he feels compelled to declare God's painful awareness of the Jews' sins, their drifting away from God's laws and their lack of repentance. At one point he describes their failure to do the right thing in these terms:

> *No-one repents of his wickedness,*
> *saying, "What have I done?"*
> *Each pursues his own course*
> *like a horse charging into battle.*
> *Even the stork in the sky*
> *knows her appointed seasons,*
> *the dove, the swift and the thrush**
> *observe the time of their migration,*
> *But my people do not know*
> *the requirements of the Lord.*

JEREMIAH
CH. 8, V. 7

* *But see the list opposite*

All these birds are indeed migrants through or to Israel. Their ability to follow natural laws created by God is in great contrast to the lack of any such ability on the part of Jeremiah's contemporaries. Modern research has revealed amazing facts about birds' migrations, such as their powers of endurance and accuracy of navigation. For example, a Swallow may leave Europe in September, fly all the way from England to South Africa, and return the following spring to the very same barn where it bred the previous year, a round trip of about 40,000 km (24,800 miles) or more.

WHITE STORK

Before we consider Jeremiah's list of birds more carefully, there is a problem with it. As already mentioned in Chapter 2, there is no universal agreement about the birds' identities and what their names should be in English. Here again is the table showing the alternatives widely used:

Authorised Version	Good News Bible	New English Bible	New Revised Standard Version	New International Version	New King James Version
stork	stork	stork	stork	stork	stork
turtle (dove)	dove	dove	Turtle Dove	dove	Turtle Dove
crane	swallow	swift	crane	swift	swift
swallow	thrush	wryneck	swallow	thrush	swallow

The first two in each list do agree. In fact, in the Holy Land, April might well be called "The month of the White Stork or Turtle Dove" because each one appears then in very large flocks on their way north. The storks certainly do arrive at "their appointed time" and walk tall and stately up to their bellies through the fields of grass or vegetables or cereals, searching for food such as grasshoppers or lizards. The doves appear in such large flocks that they seem to cover the ground to feed – it is still true today that "the voice of the Turtle Dove is heard in the land" (Song of Songs, ch. 2, vv. 12). One April, I counted around 200 in three minutes on telegraph wires by the road near Bet She'an, about 32 km (20 miles) south-east of Nazareth.

WHITE STORK

The White Stork's migration has been well studied in recent times. The routes of some individuals have been tracked by scientists who have fixed a tiny radio transmitter to each bird. They breed in Spain and Portugal, and Eastern Europe; the Iberian birds cross to Africa via Gibraltar, the eastern birds via the Bosporus into Turkey. The latter then fly on south through the Levant, the Jordan Valley in the Holy Land, into the Nile Valley, and on to their principal winter quarters from November to February in Kenya, Uganda and the eastern Cape Province of South Africa. The two populations have long been known to use these two narrow crossings, thus avoiding a long sea crossing that they dislike. These large birds, whose huge wingspan of between 155–165 cm (65–69 in) gives them plenty of "lift" but not forward speed, do need to gain a considerable height to enable them to have enough air space to progress with slow, steady wing beats and some gliding. At the two narrow crossings thermals of rising air build up as the day becomes warmer. The storks wait for these thermals to form, then rise, circling in them until they have enough height to move on. For centuries the flocks building up in August at the Bosporus have attracted the attention of tourists and scientists alike. Storks are very gregarious birds on migration, and as many as 10,000 may be seen slowly circling, rising high, before setting off south in small groups. The return in spring is the reverse of the one in autumn, but quicker – some birds may be in Russia by early April. Jeremiah wrote "seasons", and was clearly thinking of the storks in spring *and* autumn.

In 2002, The German Federal Agency for Nature Conservation published a major report, *Eastern European White Stork populations: migration studies and elaboration of conservation measures*, written by Willem Van den Bossche and four helpers. They recorded thousands of storks entering modern Israel from Syria, i.e. from the north-east and east. These flocks stop in the Jordan Valley, in the Bet She'an Valley in particular, south of the Sea of Galilee, for one night or more before moving on. The origin of 317 marked storks recovered in Israel between 1932 and 1996 are plotted on the first map opposite. The reporting of several marked birds enabled the scientists to calculate the minimal daily migration distance the birds had flown between Israel and their breeding area. One started from Israel and reached northern Germany, 3,304 km (2,053 miles) away, in 25 days, an average of 132 km (82 miles) a day. Another reached Poland 2,728 km (1,695 miles) away in 27 days, 101 km (63 miles) a day. One stork, known as Caesar, had a radio transmitter attached and was tracked every day by satellite. This enabled the ornithologists to produce an amazingly detailed map of the bird's

RINGING SITES OF WHITE STORKS RECOVERED IN ISRAEL:
DARKER SHADES DENOTE GREATER DENSITY

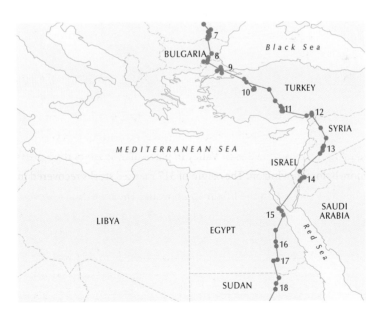

MIGRATION PATTERN OF "CAESAR", NO. 94555, FROM
BULGARIA TO SUDAN: THE NIGHT LOCATIONS ARE NUMBERED

journey as shown in the lower map opposite. It had started its migration on 26 August 1994 in northern Germany, it spent its tenth night in Turkey, was in Israel for its 14th stopover night, crossed into Egypt the next day and was well into Sudan by day 18. Another known simply by its ring number, 94549, started its migration on 1 September and was in the Bet She'an Valley on 14 September, where it stayed for 12 days. These modern observations are living evidence that it is not surprising that these large, distinctive birds attracted Jeremiah's attention. Although the Psalmist records their nesting in biblical times in Cypress Trees (Psalm 104), they have rarely nested in The Holy Land in modern times.

Turtle Doves, unlike storks, are fast fliers and usually travel at low level. Besides still being a very common migrant through Israel, these doves breed commonly in the northern and central parts of the country today. They return in April, and leave after their second brood is finished in late August or early September; large numbers from further north continue to pass through until October. These doves breed in Europe from southern England to North Africa, eastwards to Russia and the Middle East to about longitude 80° east. Eastern birds migrate today, as no doubt they did in biblical times, in flocks of hundreds or even thousands. They are exclusively vegetarian, and large numbers will drop down to feed on seeds, seedlings and leaves on the ground. Turtle Doves ringed by ornithologists in Eilat have been recovered in southern Russia at the beginning of their southward migration in August. Many Stock Doves leave Europe to winter in Israel, sometimes occurring in flocks of hundreds or even thousands.

STOCK DOVE

The next bird in Jeremiah's list is named "agur" in the Hebrew original. The most modern translations do not translate it as "crane", yet that is still the modern name – "agur afor" – for the Common Crane, and "agur hen" for the rarer Demoiselle Crane. Like the storks, they are huge, conspicuous birds on migration. They fly with long necks and legs extended, and have a wingspan of 220–245 cm (92–102 in). Often hundreds travel together in flocks. They are usually noisy as they fly on in "V" formation, keeping contact with each other, and announcing their arrival to people on the ground, with loud trumpeting calls. The commonest times to see Common Cranes in Israel are the periods of passage, September to December and March to April. Most of the birds passing through Israel are from Northern and Eastern Europe; some winter in Israel, but most fly on down the Nile Valley to winter in river valleys in Sudan and Ethiopia. These tall, grey birds are surely the species mentioned by Jeremiah. They are very conspicuous in flight and on the

COMMON CRANE

ground, and Jeremiah and his contemporaries could well have been troubled by them, as modern Israeli farmers are. From overnight roosts, flocks spread out over the fields, and although they do eat wild fruits, seeds, and some small rodents and insects, they can eat vegetables too, especially on the Sabbath when the fields are unattended. Birds that do that are bound to be noticed.

RED-RUMPED SWALLOW (TOP) AND CRAG MARTIN, SUMMER VISITORS TO ISRAEL

The fourth Hebrew name is "sus". This has been translated in times past as "swallow". But Jeremiah is quite clear that his birds are migrants, and would be more noticeable than Swallows which do winter in Israel. The Victorian naturalist in Israel, Canon Tristram, discovered that local Arab boys identified the hundreds of Swifts which were swarming about Mount Carmel and the surrounding towns and villages as "sis". The modern *Checklist of the Birds of Israel* also uses the name "sis" plus a descriptor for each of the four species that breed and pass through the country. Accompanied by screaming calls, the dramatic aerial pursuits of courting Swifts is a spectacular sight. Their "appointed time" would be clearly signalled by these black, screaming, dashing birds. The Common Swift breeds in small colonies under the eaves of houses, in holes in walls, or gaps between shutters, at a safe distance above the ground. Anyone today who visits Jerusalem or Nazareth or Tel Aviv in spring cannot fail to notice these dark, exciting birds, sometimes several species together in migrating flocks. Jeremiah must have observed them too.

Of the several members of the thrush family that occur in Israel, only the Song Thrush is common. It does not occur in large flocks, does not have vivid colours and its striking song is not commonly heard among the birds which winter in Israel. So it is not a good candidate to be in Jeremiah's list, although one of its habits may have made him aware of it – thrushes are attracted to orchards and sometimes cause damage to olives, one of the country's most important crops since ancient times. So, it seems to me that the most likely four birds in Jeremiah's list are the White Stork, Common Crane, Turtle Dove and Swift.

The other species which are also named in some translations, but with less justification, are all migrants, and which pass through Israel. The Wryneck named in the New English Bible is actually a small, brown woodpecker that feeds mainly on the ground on ants and other insects. Its shades of plumage colour make it inconspicuous, and it is generally a shy bird – not an obvious one for Jeremiah to observe often.

Ornithologists today have carefully studied in detail the migration and navigation of many birds. We know how far and how fast they can travel. They have even discovered that birds use the sun and the stars and the earth's magnetic field to navigate by. As we, and they, can and do wonder at these discoveries, there are still many questions left to answer. What makes some birds into long distance migrants, but others move no further than 1.6 km (a mile) from where they were fledged? Why are some thrushes migrants, but others are residents? To many people it is not a mystery – the birds' movements at their appointed time are part of God's plan.

CHAPTER **X**

EAGLES AND VULTURES

We have read about these birds several times already but they deserve more careful comment because they are mentioned so many times in the scriptures, especially in the Old Testament. When one gathers together several quotations for each of these birds it becomes clear that eagles and vultures were repeatedly thought of in particular ways – the eagles were given regal characteristics, but the vultures were always associated with doom and gloom.

Although these birds featured so prominently in the lives of the Jews, the Bible record is sometimes unclear as to whether it is an eagle or a vulture that is mentioned, because the word "nesher" is used for both. This is not so surprising because these huge birds are superficially alike, especially in the air high above the observer. A careful consideration of what the bird called "nesher' is doing does, however, often make it easier to distinguish between the two. Generally speaking, the eagle will be the one hunting live prey and the vulture (or more likely, vultures) will be feeding on something already dead. There is no confusion today, because the modern Hebrew has "nesher" for the Griffon Vulture and "ayit" (plus a descriptive word) for each of the eagles.

The eagle is so deeply fixed in the religion, mythology and ritual of many lands, especially Europe, North America and the Middle East, that even today many people automatically think of the eagle as the King of Birds, and that any large bird of prey is an eagle. We still speak of someone being "eagle-eyed" when he is very observant. That is a faint echo of the sympathetic magic of ancient times that enabled the power of the creature to enter the person. I have led birdwatching walks in Devon, in south-west England, and been asked, "Is that an eagle?", whereas what we were looking at was a Common Buzzard, which is the Westcountry's largest raptor but is only half the size of a Golden Eagle. To be sure of seeing one of those in the United Kingdom one must go to the Highlands of Scotland.

We do not now curse our enemies, as did our Anglo-Saxon forbears, by reciting

Under the eagle's feather
Under the eagle's claw
Ever may you wither.

Egyptian Vulture: adult below, juvenile above

In contrast, the Hebrews were part of a Middle Eastern culture which, together with their neighbours, the Babylonians, the Assyrians and the Hittites, held eagles in high esteem. Later the Romans chose it to be at the top of their legions' standards, and the Roman, scientific writer, Pliny the Elder (AD 23-79), described how many of these older nations felt about these birds: "Eagles carry the price for both honour and strength". Edward A. Armstrong, the author of *The Folklore of Birds*, regards the Middle East as the centre from which eagle traditions radiated. We call an eagle the King of Birds, perhaps without understanding why. The Hebrews did know why. Eagles were symbolic of power and they wished that the power would brush off on them, and so enable them to win in their struggles with their enemies. Unfortunately for them, that did not always work out as they wished.

A psalm of David sets the mood for the way that ideally the Jews, the men especially, would think about an eagle:

TAWNY EAGLE

Praise the Lord, O my soul;
all my inmost being, praise his holy name.
Praise the Lord, O my soul,
and forget not all his benefits -

〜 PSALM
103, vv. 1-5

who forgives all your sins
and heals all your diseases,
who redeems your life from the pit
and crowns you with love and compassion,
who satisfies your desires with good things
so that your youth is renewed like the eagle's. 〜

All these benefits – forgiveness, good health, redemption, love, compassion and feeling good – will restore a person's youthful vigour and match it to what was believed to be the unfailing strength of the eagle. The writer of the second half of Isaiah expressed the same idea many years later:

Do you not know?
Have you not heard?
The Lord is the everlasting God,
the Creator of the ends of the earth.
He will not grow tired or weary,
and his understanding no-one can fathom.

〜 ISAIAH
CH. 40, vv. 28-31

He gives strength to the weary
and increases the power of the weak.
Even youths grow tired and weary,
and young men stumble and fall;
but those who hope in the Lord
will renew their strength.
They will soar on wings like eagles;
they will run and not grow weary,
they will walk and not be faint. 〜

The characteristic of an eagle which the biblical writers repeatedly refer to, and which no doubt led to its being thought of as the source of great strength, was its flight. The writer of

Proverbs summed up the wonder that he and many others felt. Of the four things in the world he did not understand, the first was "the way of an eagle in the sky" (Proverbs, ch. 30, v. 9). Whether the "way" is where the eagle is going, for there are no tracks in the sky which show its route, or whether it is the manner in which it is managing to stay aloft so effortlessly, it is a sight which is hard to understand. It is indeed an awesome sight to see an eagle drifting, or circling on motionless wings high above the observer, or diving to capture prey. To be able to fly like an eagle was greatly to be admired and wished for, and its speed and strength were the two characteristics the Jews admired most. The late Leslie Brown, who was internationally recognized as a great expert on the lives of eagles, wrote this in 1955:

JUVENILE
TAWNY EAGLE

≈ EAGLES
CH. 2, PP. 156-157

It goes without saying that an eagle has remarkable powers of flight; were it not so the birds would not have attracted the wonder of the ancients as they did. Their powers are not those of rapid aerial evolutions, as, for instance, are possessed by the swifts and the smaller falcons, but of sustained effortless soaring flight. No bird soars with quite the same lack of effort as do the bigger birds of prey, and it has always seemed that eagles have a grace and style in the air which is not possessed by vultures, even though the latter may be even more skilled at remaining aloft for hours with a minimum of effort. At any rate, when I... have been able to examine at my leisure, for hours on end, the aerial manoeuvres of great vultures, buzzards, ravens, falcons and eagles, it has always seemed to me that the eagle has something that the others have not got – the combination of grandeur and grace. ≈

The writers of the Old Testament who watched eagles must have thought like that.

The Jews' deeply held beliefs about the eagle's power go back to their understanding of Creation. The first chapter of Genesis describes how the "Spirit of God was hovering over the waters" (Genesis, ch. 1, v. 2). This awesome and majestic picture of the way God cares for his

Creation was clearly in Moses' mind when he recited his great song of praise to "the whole assembly of Israel" near the end of his life. He recalls many great events in the nation's history, and tells the people:

Remember the days of old;
consider the generations long past...
...For the Lord's portion is his people,
Jacob his allotted inheritance.
In a desert land he found him,
in a barren and howling waste.
He shielded him and cared for him;
he guarded him as the apple of his eye,
like an eagle that stirs up its nest
and hovers over its young,
that spreads its wings to catch them
and carries them on its pinions.

DEUTERONOMY
CH. 32, VV. 7-11

BEARDED VULTURE

Moses pictures God as a protecting eagle. Eagles really are good parents. When their young are small one will stand on the nest while the other is away hunting, and will spread its wings over the chicks to shelter them from the heat of the sun or a downpour of rain so that it looks as if it is carrying them. "Hovering" may seem an odd word to describe the action of an eagle; it is a word we usually associate with the hunting technique of those small falcons, Kestrels. One of the commonest eagles in Israel today on migration and as a summer resident, and no doubt in ancient times as well, is the Short-toed Eagle. This large, impressive bird is distinctly bigger than the buzzards that would also have been seen then, and is more closely related to the harriers than the true eagles. As with most raptors the female is larger than the male, but not as great as the larger eagles. They have a wingspan of 185–195 cm (73–77 in), whereas the Golden Eagle that we might see in Europe or North America has a span of 204–220 cm (80–87 in). The most telling thing of all about the Short-toed Eagle is its characteristic ability to hang in the air, still in one spot, or to beat its great wings *to hover* as it looks for its prey, i.e. snakes: hence its other familiar name, Snake Eagle. I cannot think otherwise but that the Old Testament writers had seen this eagle, as I have. I remember one in particular, hovering with great wing beats over a leafy field of crops near the Mediterranean coast at Nasholim. The feathers under its wings and on its belly were shining white in the

STEPPE EAGLE

bright sunlight. With such a view it was easy to imagine that here was a heavenly creature, and then to go one step further and think as maybe Moses did: here was God's power in the act of overcoming the Snake of the Garden of Eden.

For the rest, the references to eagles are more likely to refer to one of the large eagles of the genus *Aquila* (to which the Golden Eagle belongs), which were and are more commonly seen in the Holy Land, such as the Steppe Eagle and the Lesser Spotted Eagle. The Steppe has a wingspan of 174–260 cm (69–102 in), but the Lesser Spotted is much smaller, with a wingspan no wider than about 160 cm (63 in).

After the deaths of King Saul and his son Jonathan, David's friend, in the battle at Mount Gilboa in 1010 BC, David followed the common practice in those times and composed a lament for the two men who had been so much part of his life. "How are the mighty fallen!" he generously cries. He then describes these two warriors with these words:

2 SAMUEL
CH. 1, V. 23

Saul and Jonathan -
in life they were loved and generous,
and in death they were not parted.
They were swifter than eagles,
they were stronger than lions.

This wonderful obituary, thanks to the King of Birds and the King of Animals, gives each of these two men a heroic stature. Sadly, an eagle's regal characteristics more often refer to Israel's enemies; they have the power and the strength and the aura of invincibility, not the sinful Jews. In about 720 BC, Hosea warned the people of the northern kingdom of Israel that they were in dire trouble:

> *Put the trumpet to your lips!*
> *An eagle is over the house of the Lord*
> *because the people have broken my covenant*
> *and rebelled against my law.*

HOSEA
CH. 8, V. 1

When we read on to verse 9 we find that the "eagle" was Assyria, which did indeed finally conquer Israel in 722–721 BC. The eagle image lived on and was repeated by later prophets. In the sixth century BC Jerusalem was described by Ezekiel as a useless vine because of the "detestable practices" of the unfaithful inhabitants. He went on to write:

> *The word of the Lord came to me; "Son of man, set*
> *forth an allegory and tell the house of Israel a*
> *parable. Say to them, 'This is what the Sovereign*
> *Lord says: a great eagle with powerful wings, long*
> *feathers and full plumage of varied colours came to*
> *Lebanon. Taking hold of the top of a cedar, he*
> *broke off its topmost shoot and carried it away to a*
> *land of merchants, where he planted it in a city of*
> *traders...But there was another great eagle with*
> *powerful wings and full plumage...[The plant] now*
> *sent out its roots towards him from the plot where*
> *it was planted and stretched out its branches to*
> *him for water.*

EZEKIEL
CH. 17, VV. 1-9

Ezekiel was one of the 10,000 or so Jews who were forced by Nebuchadnezzar into exile in Babylon in 597 BC. It was there that he wrote his prophetic book. The two great eagles were firstly King Nebuchadnezzar of Babylon, and secondly the Egyptian Pharaoh Psammetichus II or Pharaoh Hophra. Both rulers were "great eagles" and had "powerful wings" which could bring them in strength to Jerusalem. In fact, in 586 BC, Nebuchadnezzar did attack Jerusalem, breached its walls, and the city and the Temple were burned.

An eagle's swiftness is repeatedly used to describe the enemies of the Hebrews and the speed with which they bring destruction. Jeremiah who lived at this time too, saw it like this. He foresaw disaster coming from the north; the Babylonians would sweep south, led by their mighty leader:

> *Look! He advances like the clouds,*
> JEREMIAH   *his chariots come like a whirlwind,*
> CH. 4, V. 13   *his horses are swifter than eagles.*
> *Woe to us! We are ruined!*

This same eagle is recorded twice later in the prophet's emotional outburst:

> JEREMIAH   *Look! An eagle is swooping down,*
> CH. 48, V. 40   *spreading its wings over Moab.*

> JEREMIAH   *Look! An eagle will soar and swoop down,*
> CH. 49, V. 22   *spreading its wings over Bozrah.*

Moab and Edom (Bozrah is believed to have been its capital) were enemies of Judah, the southern kingdom, just east and south of the Dead Sea. The emphasis on the swooping and spreading wings suggests speed and a large size. The most common eagle in both spring and autumn migration seasons, in equally large numbers, is the Lesser Spotted Eagle. Many thousands pass through the land, with the greatest numbers in late March to early April and mid-September to mid-October. On *one* day in September as many as 46,500 have been counted flying by Kafar Kasem, north-east of Tel Aviv, on the edge of Samaria; over 100,000 have been counted passing by during the autumn en route from their breeding grounds in the Balkans, Eastern Europe and the Caucasus to their main winter quarters in Ethiopian Africa, from Sudan south to about 23° south. If we can record these huge numbers today, I believe we can be sure that the Jews of those ancient times would have been aware of these great birds, and the large numbers would have seemed like an army in the sky on the move in the autumn, sweeping down from the north – just like the invading Babylonians or Assyrians. The even larger Tawny or Steppe Eagle, with a wingspan of 180–255 cm (70–100 in) compared with the Lesser Spotted's 135–160 cm (53–63 in), is not nearly so common north of the Dead Sea. Its migration route after it passes over Eilat in southern Israel in spring and autumn in thousands, is through the valley Arava in Jordan and so on to the east of the rest of Israel. Maybe in the forty years in the Wilderness the Israelites saw these great birds in large numbers and that helped to create the pictures the prophets penned.

Two Old Testament writers, in particular Job and the author of Psalm 139, expressed a profound awareness of how awesome it is to be examined by God, to have every thought, word and deed considered by the Almighty. Both men came face-to-face with God's Creation: Job was sharply brought up to think of many aspects of it, as we have read in Chapter 6. The Psalmist, however, clearly had watched the flight of birds, because

LESSER SPOTTED EAGLE

that helped him to express how impossible it was (and is) to escape God's careful scrutiny of his life and soul:

⤳ PSALM
139, vv. 7-10

Where can I go from your Spirit?
Where can I flee from your presence?
If I go up to the heavens, you are there;
if I make my bed in the depths, you are there.
If I rise on the wings of the dawn,
if I settle on the far side of the sea,
even there your hand will guide me,
your right hand will hold me fast. ⤳

"If I rise on the wings of the dawn" poetically and beautifully seems to describe how the Psalmist cannot escape the eyes of God, even if he manages to fly high into the air like a large eagle on a thermal of rising, warm air and fly across the Sea of Galilee or the Dead Sea and land outside the Holy Land on what would be foreign territory. God will find him even there and hold him fast. The wonder of flight is under God's control, and that is one way, perhaps the best way, of understanding "the way of an eagle in the sky".

But what of vultures, the other birds that are named "nesher"? Isaiah knew these birds well, as he describes in his prophecy about the Assyrians:

> ◁ ISAIAH
> CH. 18, V. 6

They [the corpses of soldiers] will be left to
the mountain birds of prey
and to the wild animals;
the birds will feed on them all summer
the wild animals all winter. ▷

The Canadian prize-winning natural history writer, Wayne Grady, called the vulture "Nature's ghastly gourmet". Although tourists on African safaris are keen to see vultures which have been circling in the sky swoop down to the carcass of a zebra or gnu killed by lions, many are horrified by what they see closely. "They are revolting! Look at their disgusting, blood-covered, featherless heads! There's food for them all, surely, yet they are pushing and shoving and quarrelling, shoulder to shoulder." But this is the way of vultures. They are Nature's "dustbin men". They perform the essential job of clearing up the "leftovers" after the carnivores have had their fill, or of disposing of the body of a creature that has died naturally. Throughout the centuries, men and women who lived close to nature, and many who still do in Africa and India, welcome the flocks of vultures at the village middens. These people are not so squeamish as we are, who may consider them to be "ghastly gourmets". However, in many parts of India now there are no vultures, or very few, as we read in Chapter 5. These people are now realizing how much they relied on these birds, and that is how the Jews must have felt centuries ago.

The Bible does not record how useful the vultures were at keeping a village or an encampment clean. They must have served a very needful purpose in eating the offal from dressed meat and fowl prepared for the families' meal, and the entrails discarded from animals and birds at the sacrificial altar. We certainly know the latter because Abraham had to drive the vultures away from his altar (Genesis, ch. 15).

EGYPTIAN VULTURE

Bonelli's Eagle

When the Israelites were in exile in Egypt, long before they reached the Promised Land, they would certainly have been aware of vultures, both the Griffon and the less powerful Egyptian. Vultures became known as "Pharaoh's Chickens" after one Pharaoh made it a crime punishable by death to kill a vulture. He realized how important they were in a hot country to keep an area clean and healthy. Moses in particular, at the palace, would have become familiar with the way these birds were thought of, unlike the Western mind now, which still thinks rather like the American author, Gene Stratton Porter, who wrote in 1916: "I have marked the face of a vulture, when it came very close where I worked around its nest, such a look as I never saw on the face of any other bird. The age of China, the sorcery of Egypt, and the cunning of Arabia were combined in it". Something of Egypt's "sorcery" is explained in Chapter 11.

The descriptions in the Bible do not refer to vultures as being useful as Pharaoh did. Rather, when read one after the other, they seem to be like a history of the Israelites breaking God's covenant and commandments, and their punishing defeats at the hands of their enemies. This tragic history started after the death of Solomon when the country he had ruled was divided into two: the northern kingdom of Israel and the southern kingdom of Judah. The Jews' covenant with God had been described in detail (like an insurance policy!) in the book of Deuteronomy. Blessings for Obedience are listed, followed by Curses for Disobedience, in which we read:

 DEUTERONOMY
CH. 28, VV. 25-26

The Lord will cause you to be defeated before your enemies. You will come at them from one direction but flee from them in seven, and you will become a thing of horror to all the kingdoms on earth. Your carcasses will be food for all the birds of the air and the beasts of the earth, and there will be no-one to frighten them away.

The last few words are interesting because they do describe one thing that the Jews felt about birds of prey, and that would have meant vultures especially. If no person was left to scare the birds away, they would defile the bodies before there could be any mourning and the dead be given an honourable burial, according to the prescribed ritual. So the spirit of the dead would not rise to Eternal Life. The curse is exactly what happened during the reign of Jeroboam (930–909 BC). The Prophet Ahijah described the king as one who had "done more evil than all who had lived before him" (1 Kings, ch. 14, v. 9). Because of this the prophet told him:

<table>
<tr><td>

🐚 1 KINGS

CH. 14, V. 11

</td><td>

Dogs will eat those belonging to Jeroboam who die in the city, and the birds of the air will feed on those who die in the country. The Lord has spoken. 🐚

</td></tr>
</table>

Those birds of the air were surely ravens, kites – and vultures. It is interesting that the writer says the birds will not be in the city. Red and Black Kites and Ravens are still well known in many cities today. Where vultures are common they are, and presumably were, seen close by human habitation. The writer could have been thinking particularly of the soldiers who would be killed outside the city on the battlefield – they would certainly be food for the scavenging birds. Defeat like this was seen as a punishment from God, especially by the major prophets such as Isaiah, Jeremiah and Ezekiel.

Isaiah (the one who wrote Chapters 1–39) began his ministry in 740 BC. He lived mostly in Jerusalem until about 681 BC during the time of the expansion of the Assyrian empire, and predicted Judah's fall. Jeremiah began prophesying in 626 BC and went on till the fall of Jerusalem at the hands of the forces of Nebuchadnezzar in 586 BC. After that he fled to Egypt. Ezekiel was exiled to Babylon in 597 BC after Judah's defeat. He was a priest and ministered to the exiles as well as tellling them of God's wrath. All three declare God's sovereignty over all Creation and God's judgement on a sinful nation.

These grim, prophetic voices repeatedly describe how the bodies of defeated armies will be left to the birds of prey. Isaiah said so (see page 138) and Jeremiah had to be particularly blunt in reporting God's message:

<table>
<tr><td>

🐚 JEREMIAH

CH. 15, V. 3

</td><td>

"I will send four kinds of destroyers against them", declares the Lord, *"the sword to kill and the dogs to drag away and the birds of the air and the beasts of the earth to devour and destroy".* 🐚

</td></tr>
</table>

In the seventh century before Christ, a vassal treaty of Esarhaddon contained a similar curse: "May Ninurta, leader of the gods, fell you with his fierce arrow, fill the plain with your corpses, and give your flesh to the eagles and vultures to feed on". Esarhaddon was the son and successor of Sennacherib of Assyria. He ruled from 682–669 BC and was a great conqueror. Thus it was not just the Jews who knew of and recorded the work of vultures and eagles after a battle. Jeremiah expressed God's wrath in very similar words in Chapters 7 (v. 33), 16 (v. 7) and 34 (v. 20) of his book.

Black Kite

Bearded Vulture

Ezekiel was a contemporary of Jeremiah. He dated his prophetic announcements very precisely. In 587 BC, the Lord told him to "set your face against Pharaoh [Hophra] king of Egypt". Ezekiel had to declare that God "will give you as food to the beasts of the earth and the birds of the air" (Ezekiel, ch. 29, vv. 2 and 8). Similar prophecies are in chapters 32 and 34.

VULTURE

The agony of the exiles in the sixth century and the horror of the wars they had suffered was vividly expressed by the prophet's use of vultures in the descriptions of the aftermath of a battle. A particular horror for the Jews was to think that their men would not be buried according to custom. The Psalmist summed all this up in a prayer for God's forgiveness and help:

⤳ PSALM
79, vv. 1-4

O God, the nations have invaded your inheritance;
they have defiled your holy temple,
they have reduced Jerusalem to rubble.
They have given the dead bodies of your servants
as food to the birds of the air,
the flesh of your saints to the beasts of the earth.
They have poured out blood like water all around Jerusalem,
and there is no-one to bury the dead.
We are objects of reproach to our neighbours.
of scorn and derision to those around us. ⤸

The Psalmist lists the dreadful things that have happened: invasion, the Temple defiled, Jerusalem destroyed, saintly people's life-blood spilled, and the final horror is the fact that the dead were eaten by "unclean" birds and beasts and did not get a proper burial which meant that they were not prepared for the life to come.

Habbakuk, one of the minor prophets, was a contemporary of Jeremiah, and described the imminent invasion by the Babylonians. Unusually, his book is not directly a prophecy, but is more like a dialogue between himself and God. Habbakuk is very distressed by Judah's sinfulness and by God seeming to do nothing about it.

God's reply to his first complaint has a familiar vision of the future:

≈ HABBAKUK
CH. 1, VV. 8-9

[The Babylonians] are a feared and dreaded people;
they are a law to themselves
and promote their own honour.
Their horses are swifter than leopards,
fiercer than wolves at dusk.
Their cavalry gallops headlong;
their horsemen come from afar.
They fly like a vulture swooping to devour;
they all come bent on violence. ≈

What is interesting is not that the prophet repeats a description of the Babylonians' proverbial speed of attack, but that the verses are commented on in *Commentary on Habakuk* that was among the first group of scrolls found accidentally near Qumran in 1947, and now known collectively as the *Dead Sea Scrolls*. Qumran was a monastic-style settlement of the Essenes, a Jewish sect. Carbon-14 dating and palaeographic tests on the scroll indicate that this copy was written in the first century BC. The writer says of these verses: "This refers to the Kittim who trample the land with [their] horses and their beasts. From far away they come, from the seacoasts, to eat up all the peoples like an insatiable vulture" (*The Dead Sea Scrolls*, a New Translation, by Wise, Abegg Jr and Cook, p. 117).

Scholars agree that the commentator here is referring to the Romans (that is, the Kittim) who will come from overseas. They did, in 63 BC, and several years later they destroyed Qumran. About five hundred years after Habbakuk's writings, a member of the Essenes still thought the image of devouring vultures was a perfect description of the enemy. He added that he – and no doubt his contemporaries too – considered that vultures were "insatiable". Griffon Vultures are so large that their greedy feeding habits as they crowd around food are very noticeable. The word is a welcome addition to the otherwise regular comment, and is probably an observed detail about the vulture's behaviour, which the ancient authors had not described.

The final reference to these raptors is in the last book of the Bible. The vision of John the Divine was written when Christians were being persecuted by the Romans towards the end of the first century AD. He sees the Four Horsemen of the Apocalypse, who were first described by the prophet Zechariah. When John sees the White Horse and its rider, Faithful and True, the symbol of conquest, an angel appears too, who:

REVELATION
CH. 19, VV. 17-21

cried in a loud voice to all the birds flying in mid-air, "Come, gather together for the great supper of God, so that you may eat the flesh of kings, generals and mighty men, of horses and their riders, and the flesh of all people, free and slave, small and great....and all the birds gorged themselves on their flesh.

So "nature's ghastly gourmet" features in the deadly military campaigns that involved the Israelites in struggles against Egyptians, Assyrians, Babylonians and Romans. Against these nations and vultures, the King of Birds had no reply until the followers of the Christians fully understood Christ's mission, thanks to the teaching and support of such people as the writers of the Gospels, Paul and Silas, Lydia the seller of purple and John. The writer of Revelation well understood the Roman's cruel persecution because he wrote the book in wretched exile on the island of Patmos, writing in the "code" of apocalyptic literature familiar to the Jews (such as the book of Daniel), but whose true meaning would not have been understood by the Romans. John has a vision of the Throne of Heaven around which were:

REVELATION
CH. 4, VV. 6-7

four living creatures, and they were covered with eyes, in front and behind. The first living creature was like a lion, the second was like an ox, the third had a face like a man, the fourth was like a flying eagle.

Since then, as the Christian church became more established, the word of God has been spoken by readers in church at the lectern that holds the Bible. The top of that lectern on which the book rests is often a carved wooden or moulded brass eagle with outstretched wings. The writers of the four Gospels have for many centuries been depicted in art with a symbol: Matthew, a winged man; Mark, a winged lion; Luke, a winged ox; and John – the eagle.

CHAPTER **XI**

BIRDS AND WORSHIP

Many ancient cultures around the world feature birds in their art and religious rituals. Native Indians of North America, for example, put an eagle on the top of their totem poles. In Classical Greece, Athene, the goddess of wisdom, was portrayed as an owl (and the Little Owl's scientific name is now *Athene noctua*). In Australia, aborigines have wonderful creation stories in which native birds figure, such as the Australian Magpie. Early in the Christian Era, the Peacock became a symbol of immortality, and, as we have seen, the dove became a symbol of the Holy Spirit of God and of peace.

The first reference in the Bible to birds in Jewish worship is in the description of the thanksgiving Noah made to God, on the safe arrival of the Ark and his family and all the animals and birds onto dry land:

GENESIS
CH. 8, V. 20

Then Noah built an altar to the Lord and, taking some of all the clean animals and clean birds, he sacrificed burnt offerings on it. The Lord smelled the pleasing aroma...

In this description of Noah's conviction that God knew of and favourably received the sacrifice, the little detail of the "pleasing aroma" is a delightful, rather romantic, human touch. A sacrifice is similarly described elsewhere several times, in Leviticus chapter 1, for example (see page 152).

The next reference is to named birds in the story of Abraham. He received God's promise that his descendants would be as numerous as the stars, and he would inherit the Promised Land. Abraham felt he had to seal his agreement with a religious ceremony, and so he prepared a sacrifice. He slaughtered "a heifer, a goat, a ram, each three years old, along with a dove and a young pigeon" (Genesis, ch. 15, v. 9).

Many years later, in historical times, when the Israelites were in exile in Egypt, Moses in particular, at Pharaoh's court, would have become familiar with how birds were a rich part of religious life there. The Egyptians over the years believed in several gods, whom they represented by birds. The goddess Nekhebt was depicted by a Griffon Vulture (see page 20). The god of knowledge, Thoth, was represented by the Sacred Ibis. A carving of the ibis was used as a votive offering, and mummified ibises were buried in many different catacombs as late as the Ptolemaic times (c.350–30 BC). The god Horus was the guardian of the ruler. His bird is the falcon (or

LITTLE OWL

PEREGRINE: ADULT BELOW, JUVENILE ABOVE

hawk) whose wings are often shown spread protectively over the Pharaoh's picture. Some representations are clearly a falcon, probably a Peregrine, but in the Late Period, a tomb at Saqqara was specially built for mummified Horus-falcons, which, in fact, were actually several different birds of prey.

The Israelites were not moved to follow their Egyptian masters and believe in the divine power of these birds – at least, we are not told they did. They did early on in their escape from Egypt complain about the hardships they were enduring in the desert; they did build an idol of a golden calf while they were impatiently waiting for Moses to return from his talk with God, but were eventually set back on the straight and narrow by the Ten Commandments, and God's command:

Do not make any gods to be alongside me; do not make yourselves gods of silver or gods of gold. Make an altar of earth for me and sacrifice on it your burnt offerings and fellowship offerings, your sheep and goats and your cattle. Wherever I cause my name to be honoured, I will come to you and bless you.

EXODUS
CH. 20, VV. 23-24

The Israelites, through the centuries, did fail God several times by not obeying His commands. Initially in the Promised Land they had an altar "at a high place" at each of their settlements. At first, each head of the household performed the holy ritual, but as the years went by, priests increasingly took control; priests who could trace their ancestry back to Aaron and the sacrifices were concentrated in Jerusalem. Here, eventually, a great, permanent Temple was built on the orders of Solomon.

The birds, which were part of the sacrificial ceremony through the centuries, were the same as in Abraham's day, but the laws controlling the act were carefully laid down in several chapters of Leviticus. There were five types of sacrifice one could make. Three were voluntary: the Burnt Offering, the Grain Offering and the Fellowship Offering; two were mandatory: the Sin Offering and the Guilt Offering. The second was in recognition of God's goodness and the offering was grain, olive oil, flour, baked bread or salt. The participants in all the others had to bring an animal without any defect such as a bull, a ram or a goat; but the poor could bring a dove or a young pigeon as a Burnt Offering or a Sin Offering.

The Law had very precise instructions in it, describing how the birds were to be part of the sacrificial ceremony:

 LEVITICUS
CH. 1, VV. 14-17

If the offering to the Lord is a burnt offering of birds, he is to offer a dove or a young pigeon. The priest shall bring it to the altar, wring off the head and burn it on the altar; its blood shall be drained out on the side of the altar. He is to remove the crop with its contents and throw it to the east side of the altar, where the ashes are. He shall tear it open by the wings, not severing it completely, and then the priest shall burn it on the wood that is on the fire on the altar. It is a burnt offering, an offering made by fire, an aroma pleasing to the Lord.

The doves were most likely hand-reared birds like the pigeons kept in lofts and dovecotes around the world today. They were first bred long ago from wild Rock Doves, as we have already read. It is possible that in Palestine in biblical times migrant Turtle Doves were trapped and sold. The whole point of the sacrifice was to appease God, to be "in his good books" again, and to obtain remission for sins committed. This action was clearly emphasized by the prophet Ezekiel:

EZEKIEL
CH. 45, V. 15

Also one sheep is to be taken from every flock of two hundred from the well watered pastures of Israel. These will be used for the grain offerings, burnt offerings and fellowship offerings to make atonement for the people, declares the Sovereign Lord.

Many clans and peoples and nations around the world and through the ages have had a belief that blood is a mysterious fluid that is the basis of life. This close association with life means that blood was, and is, thought of as sacred to many people, and can be used only as the proper gift to God, the Creator of Life. It is thus at one and the same time the perfect gift at the altar and the most potent symbol of the worshipper's desire to show his or her devotion to God, and the desire to be forgiven for any sin, to feel clean; indeed, Jewish Law prescribed a sacrificial gift as a thanksgiving after a skin disease had been healed:

TURTLE DOVE

If the person has been healed of his infectious skin disease, the priest shall order that two live clean birds and some cedar wood, scarlet yarn and hyssop be brought for the one to be cleansed. Then the priest shall order that one of the birds be killed over fresh water in a clay pot. He is then to take the live bird and dip it, together with the cedar wood, the scarlet yarn and the hyssop, into the blood of the bird that was killed over the fresh water. Seven times he shall sprinkle the one to be cleansed of the infectious disease and pronounce him clean. Then he is to release the live bird in the open fields.

⟿ LEVITICUS
CH. 14, VV. 3-7

The live bird being released reminds us of the instruction for a Sin Sacrifice (Leviticus, ch. 16) when of the two goats taken to the altar, one had to be killed and the other released covered in the blood of the other: the one pays the price of the sin and the other goes off bearing the sin, hence the term we sometimes hear today – he's a scapegoat!

Elsewhere in the Law we read that Cedar, yarn and hyssop were used in cleansing ceremonies. Perhaps the yarn on a stick was used to sprinkle the blood. Hyssop is a small bushy aromatic herb and the name has long been used to name the plant used in the ceremony; in the Holy Land it is most probably the Caper which is a symbol of endurance and strength: "Cleanse me with hyssop," said the Psalmist, "and I shall be clean" (Psalm 51, v.7).

These references to blood also explain why Jews then and now do not eat blood products, and all animals and birds must be carefully slaughtered and the meat specially prepared. It must be "kosher":

LEVITICUS

CH. 17, vv. 10-14

Any Israelite or alien living among them who eats any blood - I will set my face against that person who eats blood and will cut him off from his people. For the life of a creature is in the blood, and I have given it to you to make atonement for yourselves on the altar; it is the blood that makes atonement for one's life. Therefore I say to the Israelites, "None of you may eat blood, nor may an alien among you eat blood Any Israelite or any alien living among you who hunts any animal or bird that may be eaten must drain out the blood and cover it with earth, because the life of every creature is its blood; anyone who eats it must be cut off".

As the years went by, the spiritual and devotional aspect of sacrifice was lost on some people. The confining of worship and sacrifice to the Temple in Jerusalem meant that big business grew up in the large, outer area of the temple called the Court of the Gentiles, an area of several acres. At times of festivals, hundreds of pilgrims would be thronging the Temple Mount, and needing to buy an animal or birds for the family sacrifice. The "supermarket" of stalls had become so big in Jesus' time it led to one of the best-known stories in the Gospels:

ST MARK
CH. 11, VV. 15-17

On reaching Jerusalem, Jesus entered the temple area and
began driving out those who were buying and selling there.
He overturned the tables of the money-changers and the
benches of those selling doves, and would not allow anyone
to carry merchandise through the temple courts. And as he
taught them, he said, "Is it not written:
'My house will be called
a house of prayer for all nations'.
But you have made it a den of robbers."

TURTLE DOVE

DOVE OF PEACE

Jesus' angry cry is a direct quotation from the prophet Isaiah (ch. 56, v. 7). Far from being a place which led to where the nation had come to worship, the outer court had become a noisy, and no doubt smelly, market place. The Temple had been robbed of its sanctity, and the pilgrims fleeced of their hard-earned money. Despite the rightness of Jesus' anger, the priests and teachers of the law feared His teaching and His appeal to the crowds in Jerusalem who had come to give homage at the feast of the Passover.

In the midst of all the mayhem that day the purpose and symbolism of the doves was lost. Gone were the symbols of peace and the Spirit of God. When Jesus saw the doves in their cages perhaps He thought of the words of the Psalmist: "Do not hand over the life of your dove to wild beasts" (Psalm 74, v.19) which speaks of the dove's helplessness in the hands of the money-making salesmen. It was hard that day to see the innocence of doves (St Matthew, ch. 10, v. 16) which is how the disciples had to be when they went out to preach the Good News, or to see "the Spirit of God descending like a dove" and alighting on Jesus (St Matthew, ch. 3, v. 16).

Sacrifices such as these seem very gruesome to us so used to the often quiet, reflective or colourfully robed, musical Christian services. To the Jews the Burnt Offering was an act of devotion, commitment and surrender to God's will which was as important to them as baptism, or a Confirmation blessing from a bishop, or partaking Holy Communion are to a Christian. It was mandatory to offer a sacrifice to atone for a specific sin, and to seek forgiveness and cleansing for that sin. Whoever you were, and whatever creature was sacrificed, it cost you. Sometimes today people lose sight of that cost in Christian worship. As the congregation sits in church the people do not as clearly and as visually demonstrate their surrender to God's will. Mary and Joseph, when they took Jesus to the Temple in Jerusalem, and made their sacrifice of two doves, were not only worshipping as the Law in Leviticus chapter 8 demanded, but were also publicly declaring their love of God.

Of all the mentions of the many species of birds in the Bible, the most important then, are those of the dove. The dove helped Noah in the beginning, doves were a vital part of sacrificial worship, the dove was the symbol of the Holy Spirit at Christ's baptism, and today, worldwide, a white dove is the symbol of peace. May that bird fly more strongly as the days go by.

FURTHER READING

Armstrong, Edward A.	1958	*The Folklore of Birds*
Baly, Denis	1959	*The Geography of the Bible*
Brown, Leslie	1955	*Eagles*
Cottridge, D., Porter, R.	2000	*A Photographic Guide to Birds of Israel and the Middle East*
Hadoram, Shirihai	1996	*The Birds of Israel*
Hovel, Haim	1987	*Checklist of the Birds of Israel*
Mullarney, Killian et al	1999	*Collins Bird Guide*
Parmelee, Alice	1959	*All the Birds of the Bible*
Paz, Uzi	1987	*The Birds of Israel*
Porter, Richard et al.	2010	*Field Guide to the Birds of the Middle East, revised 2nd edition*
Reid, Carlton	1993	*Berlitz: Discover Israel*
Stott, Rev. John	1999	*The Birds Our Teachers - essays in orni-theology*
Stratton-Porter, Gene	1916	*Birds of the Bible*
Tristram, Rev. H.B.	1867	*The Natural History of the Bible*
	1884	*Fauna and Flora of Palestine*

All Bible quotations are from *The NIV Study Bible: New International Version* (1998 edition). of the International Bible Society, unless otherwise stated.

Quotes from the Good News Bible © 1994 published by the Bible Societies/HarperCollins Publishers Ltd UK, Good News Bible© American Bible Society 1966, 1971, 1976, 1992.

Other Bible quotations about the birds we have studied can be found at several websites such as www.studylight.org on the Holman Bible Dictionary page "Birds".

ACKNOWLEDGEMENTS

I suppose it was inevitable that as a Methodist Local Preacher and a lifelong birdwatcher I was going to put the two disciplines together – and this book is the result of many years' pondering. Once I thought I had done all I could, I felt I needed to have the Bible content and interpretation looked at by other churchgoers. In particular, I am very grateful to three fellow preachers, who spent time reading and commenting on the manuscript: Kathy Brown, Roger Aldersley and Judith Allen. I welcomed their suggestions and their help gave me confidence to finish. The bird information is based on my own experience and reading. I hope that what you read helps you better to appreciate what the writers of the Old and New Testaments had in mind when they named a bird.

INDEX

B

Bee-eater 11, 84, 118
Bittern 40, 111
Blackbird 101
Blackstart 104
Bulbul, Yellow-vented 17, 84, 101, 104
Bullfinch 104
Bustard 102
Bustard, Houbara 103
Buzzard 25, 38, 111, 132, 133
Buzzard, Common 72, 120, 128
Buzzard, Honey 25

C

Canary 18, 104
Chukar 51, 52, 113
Cockerel 87
Cormorant 22, 29, 30, 40, 111
Cormorant, Great 22, 40
Cormorant, Pygmy 22, 40
Crane 21, 23, 121, 124
Crane, Common 125, 124, 127
Crane, Demoiselle 124
Crow 30, 43, 85, 88
Cuckoo 46, 52, 98
   Pallid 104

D

dove, cooing 16, 17, 84, 98, 101, 103
   for sacrifice 81, 84, 148, 152
   in the fields 101
   in worship 148–157
   the Spirit of God 82, 83, 84, 148, 157
Dove, Collared 50, 103
   Laughing 50, 112
   Mourning 103
   Palm 101, 104
   Rock 49, 60, 61, 101, 104, 112, 152
   Stock 49, 50, 66
   Turtle 23, 49, 50, 62, 84, 98, 101, 103, 112, 121, 124, 127, 152

E

Eagle 6, 15, 29, 30, 31, 33, 71, 72, 76, 78, 84, 94, 112, 120, 128–47
   Golden 33, 128, 133, 134
   Lesser Spotted 33, 137
   Short-toed 25, 133
   Snake 31, 133
   Steppe 33, 134, 137
   Tawny 130, 145
Egret, Cattle 42
   Little 29, 40

F

Falcon 20, 25, 30, 38, 39, 72, 93, 111, 112, 120, 132, 133, 149, 151
finch 88, 98
Francolin, Black 51

G

Geese 19, 46, 49, 116
Goldfinch 98, 104
Grackle, Tristram's 18, 19
Greenfinch 101
Guineafowl, Helmeted 46
Gull 24, 29, 40
Gull, Black-headed 40
   Herring 40
   Lesser Black-backed 40

H

Hawk 29, 30, 38, 72, 79, 111, 119, 120, 151
Heron 19, 21, 24, 29, 30, 40, 42
Heron, Grey 96
Hoopoe 11, 19, 24, 29, 30, 40, 43, 65, 84

I

Ibis, Glossy 74
   Sacred 19, 20, 92, 149

J

Jay 85
Junglefowl, Red 44, 45

K

Kestrel, Common 104
    Lesser 104, 111
Kingfisher 84, 98
Kite 24, 29, 30, 37, 62, 142
Kite, Black 29, 37, 142
    Red 29, 37

L

Lammergeier 36
Lark 84, 88, 98
Lark, Crested 97

N

Nightjar 25

O

Osprey 25, 29, 30, 40, 114
Ostrich 74, 75, 76, 111
Owl 16, 21, 31, 37, 38, 72, 73, 102, 103, 104, 111, 148
Owl, Barn 38
    Desert 29, 30, 37, 38, 102, 111
    Eagle 38, 103
    Fisher 25, 30
    Great 29, 37, 111
    Horned 29, 30, 38, 102
    Little 24, 25, 29, 30, 38, 148
    Long-eared 24, 30, 38
    Scops 38
    Screech 24, 25, 29, 30, 37, 38, 102, 111
    Short-eared 24, 25, 30, 38
    Tawny 24, 30, 38, 102
    White 29

P

Partridge 49, 53, 52
Partridge, Sand 51
Peacock 22, 98, 148
Peregrine 20, 38, 151
Pheasant 15, 45, 51, 52
Pigeon 28, 38, 49, 50, 51, 60, 61, 81, 80, 148, 151, 152
Pigeon, Wood 49, 50
Prinia, Graceful 84

Q

Quail 49, 51, 53, 54

R

Raven 6, 21, 24, 29, 30, 37, 40, 43, 58, 60, 62, 66, 67, 76, 98, 102, 111, 132, 142
Raven, Brown-necked 43, 67
    Common 43, 67
    Fan-tailed 43, 67

S

Sandgrouse, Black-bellied 55
    Pintailed 55
Serin, Tristram's 18
Shrike 19, 85
Sparrow 20, 85, 86, 97, 110
Sparrow, House 84, 86, 88, 111
Sparrowhawk, Levant 120
Stork 17, 23, 24, 29, 30, 40, 74, 106, 118, 120, 121, 122, 124
Stork, White 40, 106, 121, 122, 127
Swallow 17, 19, 21, 23, 84, 110, 111, 116, 118, 121, 126, 127
Swallow, Barn 111, 116
    Red-rumped 104,
Swan 21, 22, 93
Swift 23, 84, 101, 118, 120, 121, 127, 132
Swift, Common 127
Sunbird, Palestine 84, 101

T

Tit, Great 101
Thrush 23, 120, 121, 127,
Thrush, Song 127

V

Vultures 20, 21, 23, 29, 31, 35, 33, 34, 36, 62, 67, 76, 78, 86, 87, 128–147
    Bearded 24, 30, 36, 37
    Black 25, 29, 30, 31, 34
    Egyptian 25, 62
    Griffon 20, 24, 30, 34, 62, 65, 78, 84, 128, 146, 148
    Lappet-faced 34
    Ruppell's 109

W

Warbler, Graceful 84
Wryneck 121, 127